THINK BIG AND KICK ASS IN POLITICS

*HOW A REPUBLICAN BILLIONAIRE
MASTERMINDED HIS WAY INTO THE WHITE HOUSE*

NICCOLÒ DAVINCI

Order this book online at www.trafford.com
or email orders@trafford.com

Most Trafford titles are also available at major online book retailers.

Print information available on the last page.

ISBN: 978-1-4907-7649-1 (sc)
ISBN: 978-1-4907-7650-7 (hc)
ISBN: 978-1-4907-7651-4 (e)

Library of Congress Control Number: 2016913846

Trafford rev. 08/25/2016

www.trafford.com
North America & international
toll-free: 1 888 232 4444 (USA & Canada)
fax: 812 355 4082

Contents

Dedication

To Donald Trump, the illustrious mastermind. Also, to Robert Greene, Herman Cain, Jay-Z and every other brainiac out there—male, female, etc.—with the ability to decipher masterful political strategy. You all inspire me, like kerosene that whispers to a perpetually burning flame. It is time to reclaim our throne. America WILL be great again! Believe it!

Acknowledgments

Frist, I would like to thank two of the world's greatest strategists, Sun Tzu and Niccolò Machiavelli, for pioneering the strategic platform that has birthed the principles that govern modern politics. Without it, the game of power in America would not even exist. And I also thank author Robert Greene for carrying the strategic torch and, most importantly, passing it on to the modern generation. *The Art of War, The Prince, The 48 Laws of Power, The Art of Seduction* and *Mastery* are much more than intriguing works to be perused. Collectively, they constitute the lifeblood of not only America and the world, but also human life and practical human reasoning. These works play an essential role in my way of thinking concerning power and the political process, and without them, this book would have only remained a dream.

Secondly, I must also send an abundance of thanks to all of my enemies, who inspire me more than my friends. The nefarious lies, infantile games, subtle manipulation, jealousy and devious skepticism that comprise your behavioral existence are what, in many ways, *made* this book possible. Therefore, I thank you all for your inspiration, and look forward to *demolishing* you on life's battlefield. *¡Bésame el trasero!*

On a personal note, thirdly, I send my gratitude to CNN reporter Rosa Flores, for unknowingly inspiring me to pursue authorship on a greater level during our brief time together in Louisiana. Her innate passion, poise, elegant stoicism and impartiality motivated me to broadly expand my worldview on numerous subjects. And, for that, to her, I am deeply indebted. Thanks!

I also send gratitude to Trafford Publishing, for helping me bring the truth herein to a society that inherently hungers for answers, as well as change. To Senior Publishing Consultant Shannon Andrews, thank you *so* much for your kindness, patience and heartfelt inspiration. Working with you has been a joy from the beginning and, one day, the universal reward for your compassion will manifest in abundance. And, to my great friend, and *brother*, "Romain," for being one of the *biggest* thinkers I have ever known. Your intelligence, audacity, pragmatic worldview and manifold skills and talents keep me focused on the bigger picture when it seems as if the chips are down and I am falling off my game. Your own resilience propels me to bounce back every time, and I love you more than you will ever know. The world is yours to conquer, and soon enough, society will realize the importance of Katana Solutions!

And, lastly, to my beautiful wife, Sheron, what is understood need not be explained. I *love* you!

Author's Note

In every era, a mastermind comes along who, through shrewd strategy, confounds the minds of those in society. And this master's mind is usually a paradox; his or her behavior, even more of a mystery. However, in the same era, eventually, a "mastermind master" also comes along. While the majority is on pins and needles trying to figure out the former, the latter possesses a tremendous gift of boundless insight that turns the unfathomable into non-transparency. Some could call this kind of person a "decipherer," one who can see the unseen and simplify it for public understanding. The author is such a person. If you are reading this book, then, this means that you are no fool. Whether you love or hate Donald Trump, he obviously intrigues you—or simply pisses you off. Whatever it is, the point is that you seek to understand him. Well, you have come to the right place! In this book, the author leaves no stone unturned. He takes you into the mind and strategy of Trump in a way that has never been done before and, by the time you finish it, whether you like Trump or not, you will have learned to respect The Donald. I have done my best to make this book as straightforward, fun and easygoing as possible. I KNOW you will enjoy it. So, kick back, free your mind and relish the secret to kick-ass politics. In this way, you will really see how Donald Trump is making America great again!

"Any man who tries to be good all the time is bound to come to ruin among the great number who are not good. Hence a prince who wants to keep his authority must learn how to not be good, and use that knowledge, or refrain from using it, as necessity requires."

The Prince, *Niccolò Machiavelli*

Introduction

Power is a social game, and if you truly want to understand Republican billionaire Donald Trump, my advice to you is to scratch everything that you think you know about politics and focus on what you know about *power* and the general rules or principles that govern the game. We are no longer living in an age where political correctness seems absolute. The political dynamic is changing, America is falling, and The People are fed up. Hence, the time has now come for mass social awakening, and understanding the Trump Train is what will help us make America great again!

In society, there are only three kinds of people: the powerful, the power aspirants and the powerless. "They" tell you this in another language when they mention the upper, middle and lower classes. But, at the end of the day, it is all about *power*. In one way or another, *everybody* wants it, and only powerful people make powerful decisions that can create positive change in not just America, but the world. You can deny this if you want to, but you would only be lying to yourself. In order for large-scale change to occur in any society, a certain mindset is needed, and this mindset has to be guided by profound wisdom, flat out common sense and sheer understanding of masterful strategy. "They" call it the "It Factor." *I* call it the "Mastermind Mindset," or "Double M," for short. And, guess what—Trump's got it! If you disagree, then, I dare you to truly ponder on and answer the following questions:

If Donald Trump Does *Not* Have the "Double M," Then…

- Why have all of his political opponents fallen at his feet?
- Why can't anyone figure out his political strategy?
- Why hasn't he been stopped yet?

- Why is he appealing to so many voters, and just people in general?
- Why is he a self-made, multibillion-dollar powerhouse?
- And why are we even *talking* about him so goddamn much?

If you were to honestly answer these questions and impartially evaluate your answers, your own findings would point to the fact that Trump *definitely* has the Mastermind Mindset. He or she who denies this has the mind of a rock and the perspicacity of a donkey. Even a child could see and understand that all of the above is what happens when a *true* mastermind hits the scene.

The point is that Donald Trump is *kicking ass* in politics and, by strategic appearance, masterfully masterminding his way into the White House. And I say this with no negative undertone or connotation. Every man who has ever become President became so by *masterminding* his way into that position. The same is true of virtually all of the ancient kings, queens and pharaohs that we have heard and read about in world history, and we also see signs of the same in business and entertainment all the time. Strategy and power go hand in hand, and politics, my friend, is nothing but *strategy*. Once you take emotion out of the equation and see things for what they really are, it becomes virtually *impossible* to hate Donald Trump.

With that said, so that there will be no misunderstanding, let me tell you what this book is about, exactly.

The Un-Equivocal Book Breakdown

Just as the title says, this book is about thinking BIG and kicking ass in politics. More specifically, it is about how *Donald Trump* is kicking ass in the political arena, how *you* can kick ass in the same, and how I believe, based on my own findings and gut instincts, that Trump is shrewdly *masterminding* his way into the White House. I wrote it for those of you who, like me, are fascinated by power, politics and entertainment—as well as those who simply cannot understand The Donald. However, it is also written for those still-undecided voters who have the power to help change the nation by going to the ballot box, and for others who are seeking power-based progress in their respective fields. Whatever you are looking for, you will definitely find it here.

In Chapter 1, "Trump and *The 48 Laws of Power*: Mastery at Its Finest," I take you into the mind of Donald Trump to show you just how shrewd of a power player he truly is when it comes to strategy and politics. By the end of this chapter, there should be no doubt in your mind about him being a master of the power game.

In Chapter 2, "The Machiavellian Mindset: Princes and Peasants," I dabble into Niccolò Machiavelli's political treatise, *The Prince*, to show you the key differences between masterminds and conventionalists. But I also question the social concept of morality and point out how *true* political reasoning has turned Donald Trump into a modern-day Machiavelli. You will also read about what I call the "Modern Age of the Cyclops."

Chapter 3, "Politics and *The Art of Seduction*: What the Public *Really* Wants," discusses the importance of seduction in power and politics, and reveals the roles that we have all played in actually *helping* Trump rise to the top politically—whether we like him and intended to, or not. It also lets us social dwellers know what we want, even if we do not even know so ourselves.

As for Chapter 4, "America and the Art of War: Have We *Really* Forgotten?" it is a reality check that serves as a reminder of what political warfare truly is, and how the powerful among us have dropped the political ball. I hope that this chapter inspires us to pick it back up. Additionally, this chapter is an inspirational piece for those of you who aspire to *become* powerful and successful. In order to acquire such and maintain it, one has to, at least, know and understand the basic principles of which power consists. This chapter, in brief, tells all.

Chapter 5 is all about thinking BIG in order to be where you want to be in life, politics included. This chapter, entitled "The *Real* Power of the Law of Attraction: Only the *Hungriest* Will Survive," demonstrates how extraordinarily BIG thinking pushed Donald Trump from Trump Tower to the White House. It also reveals how, at the end of the day, the small thinking of Trump's political opponents resulted in their *own* defeat. This chapter teaches you how *not* to make the same mistake. If you want power, or already have it but want to augment and maintain it, this is *definitely* a chapter I suggest you read.

In Chapter 6, "Only Knowledge Applied *Shrewdly* Equals Power: Ill-Wisdom of the Ages," I discuss how clever application of *practical* "common sense" is much more powerful than worn-out strategies and political correctness. Specifically, this brief chapter touches on how age-old wisdom *inhibits* power and shows you how, in real life as well as formal politics, it is not about what and who you know, but rather what you do or do *not* do, that will make you successful. And Trump is definitely *doing* it!

In Chapter 7, I divert from politics for a bit to discuss a topic that almost always comes up whenever a mastermind pops up on a particular scene and does the seemingly impossible. This topic is the much-lauded, secret society group known as the "Illuminati." In this chapter, "Assassination and the Illuminati: Where *Trump* Fits into the Equation," in spite of what conspiracy theorists are saying about Trump being an Illuminati member, and him eventually being targeted for assassination by the same group, I paint a different picture that reveals how superior *strategy*, not secret societal membership, is the cause of Trump's success. This chapter re-establishes the truth about Trump—a truth that is rarely found in the hub of theoretical conspiracy on YouTube.

The newest social perspective regarding modern politics is discussed in Chapter 8, entitled "A Wake-up Call for America: Revision of the Political Dynamic." This chapter asserts that Trump, foreseeing the latest evolution in contemporary politics, used strategy to his advantage in order to propel himself to the forefront of the Republican Party in 2016. It makes it pretty obvious that, after Trump, the standard American blueprint for political power will *never* be the same. It also explains how Trump would *still* come out a winner if he loses the 2016 election.

And, lastly, Chapter 9, the final chapter, is all about *you*. In this section, entitled "*You* Can Be a Political Mastermind Too: The Formula, Step-by-Step," I give you a practical formula for political and general success that can make your rise to the top more real than you could ever imagine. After reading this chapter, if you are *really* serious about having the "Double M," the Mastermind Mindset, you will walk away from this book thinking BIG and inspired to go kick some ass—in the political mastermind sense, of course. You will understand the politics of life, as opposed to the simple politics of state, and how, in your quest for power, the former will get you much further than the latter. I also expose hush-hush information about TV star Mimi Faust from VH1's hit reality show, *Love & Hip Hop: Atlanta*, that will have fans on the edges of their seats, at a complete lost for words. If you are looking for a practical blueprint for power, this is *definitely* it.

People ask me all the time, "Why are you supporting Donald Trump?" "Do you really believe that he would be good for America?" My typical response to these people normally goes as follows: "The *real* question is, 'Why are you *not* supporting him?' And, please, tell me how a BIG-thinking, *master* strategist with a proven track record of *making* success happen would *not* be good for America." And I have yet to meet anyone who could respond to me without leaving social conditioning and emotion out of the equation. They are either anti-Trump due to their political and religious affiliations (conditioned), or still pissed off at him because of some comment he once made (emotional). They know next to nothing about strategy, so they never see the big picture. They are too busy thinking small, and the only ass that they are used to kicking is their own. Unless they change their thinking from small to BIG, people like this will *always* lose. But Donald Trump is a BIG thinker, shrewd mastermind and *winner*! This, at the very least, is why I support him and dedicate this book to his name.

But here is something ironic. Many years ago, when I was still caught up in the Social Matrix, like so many others who are still trapped in that illusion, I used to think that Donald Trump was a complete asshole. But, one day, after seeing him on TV, something in my gut told me that I was wrong about him. So, I started researching him. The more I read, the more I respected him. Then, around 2010, while working as a librarian and overdosing on Rhonda Byrne's book *The Secret*, I came across what Jack Canfield once said was "Donald Trump's version of *The Secret*": a profoundly inspiring book that Trump co-authored with Bill Zanker, entitled *Think Big and Kick Ass in Business and Life*. In retrospect, I can honestly say that this book changed my life forever. I recently found a copy in my wife's library and have not been able to put it down since.

But I said all of that to say this: If you are one of those people who thinks that Donald J. Trump is an asshole who is unfit to be President, you are sadly mistaken and, nine times out of ten, with all due respect, your mind is still caught up in the Social Matrix. Instead of judging the man, I challenge you to put your racial, religious and state-based, political pride aside and take time out to understand him. If you truly believe in your country and want to help create change that will make America better for all citizens, you can begin by reading this book. This is the first step. Do not make the mistake that I made by thinking small, because we can only make America and ourselves great by thinking BIG! Hell with what critics are saying about Trump, because they are not winning—he is. So, obviously, we know that he is doing *something* right. Kicking ass is just a part of life, and I do not know about you, but I *love* it! If you are not where you want to be in life, or currently on the pathway leading in that direction, then, apparently, you are not thinking BIG enough and acting on those thoughts. But Trump is. How can you not respect him for that?

Are you a fool or a thinker? A coward or a fighter? Do you want to think BIG, or think small? And, if you are not *winning* enough, are you not tired of getting your ass kicked? The point is that masterminds read *books* about masterminds; by mastering strategy, you master *power*; and, by understanding strategy *and* power, you will understand Donald Trump. The presidential primaries are over. At the ballot box, your vote matters. This shit is *real* now. Where we go from here is simply your decision. And, though he has a pretty amazing shot at winning, even if Trump does *not* win the 2016 presidential election, he will, undoubtedly, continue to think BIG and kick ass in politics, business and life—and you can do the same. With that said, turn the page, read this book—and go kick some ass!

Niccolò DaVinci

1

Trump and The 48 Laws of Power: Mastery at Its Finest

Every person on the face of this planet, in one way or another, is bound to a particular way of thinking, and a set of principles, that guide their actions. If most people were able to understand this, they would spend less time judging and trying to figure out others, and more time doing their own thing, because they would already realize that people are going to do whatever they want to do regardless. Their thinking patterns lead them to do so. But the truth is that most people will never reach this level of thinking. If they ever do, it definitely will not be any time soon. Why? Because their concept of what is right and wrong prevents them from doing such. In the very real world that we live in, they *choose* to not see and acknowledge the truth about people, and use everything from religion to generational misconceptions and excuses to justify their views on morality and life. When things go wrong, they run, too afraid to face their fears and challenge their own conditioned minds. When people harm, betray and threaten to hurt them, instead of striking back, they retreat, like cowards. To these kinds of people, revenge is "evil." They say things, like, "I don't have time for this negative energy" or "I'll just go pray about it." And it is exactly this particular mindset that makes them completely unequipped to even *participate* in the game of power, much more succeed at it. They pray to their gods but still end up getting fucked over in life. And I see examples of this every single day. You do, too—unless you are just in denial.

The truth is that Jesus is not coming back any time soon and, as much as you may *want* the world to be peaceful, this will not happen any time soon, either. People are going to rob, steal and kill until the world is over. They will deceive you, if you let them. They will lie to you as if it is nothing, befriend you and, then, stab you in the back, with no remorse. This is just life. Take it or leave it. If you want to have power or be successful in *real*-life "politics," you have to understand this first and accept that it all just comes with the territory. If you can understand this, soon enough, you will realize that life itself is nothing but a hub of political chaos. And, believe me, Donald Trump *definitely* understands this.

If you are not familiar with the works of Robert Greene by now, and have little to no idea of whom Sun Tzu and Niccolò Machiavelli were, and power is what you want, be it political or otherwise, it is time for you to step up your game. We live in the Information Age, so I need not go into profound detail about these amazing men. Your Web browser exists for that purpose. But let me give you the basics.

Sun Tzu was an ancient Chinese general, military strategist and philosopher. Greene is a bestselling author, speaker and acclaimed authority on strategy, power and seduction. And Niccolò Machiavelli, a late "distant relative" of mine, is credited as being "the founder of modern political science." Although strategy and power were being exercised long before these men ever existed, they studied and documented it in comprehensive, guidebook form, which, to this very day, facilitates one's application of strategy while on the quest for power. Countless people who have risen to power have pointed to their works, referencing them as political bibles, so to speak. And this is exactly what they are: political bibles on strategy and power. Hence, I, too, reference them. Just as every serious Christian should have a Holy Bible—and every Muslim, a Holy Quran—every person seeking success in politics, business and life should have copies of these men's works. Chiefly, *The Art of War* (Sun Tzu), *The Prince* (Machiavelli) and *The 48 Laws of Power* (Greene). And they should study and apply the knowledge within these works as if their lives depended on it. In the power game, believe me, your life surely does.

Now, in the Introduction, I mentioned that Donald Trump is a mastermind. I also asserted that, by strategic appearance, he is "masterfully masterminding his way into the White House." And guess what—I meant every word of it. And I believe that, if you read the three books I just mentioned, with emphasis on *The 48 Laws of Power*, you will see Donald Trump written all over them. Therefore, so that you can see this for yourself, in this chapter, I will review the 48 Laws and show you how, in my opinion, Trump is applying them as he sees fit—all to his advantage. If you have paid enough attention to him in the media, it will not be hard for you to see how masterfully he exercises these Laws. Moreover, if you do not have a copy of *The 48 Laws of Power*, then, I suggest you acquire one. With that said, let us begin.

Law 1
Never Outshine the Master

As we all know, anyone in a position above someone else is superior to the person positioned below. And he or she that is superior is *master*. Therefore, when a non-superior person aims to surpass a superior, the worst thing that he or she can do is outshine the master. Doing so would only, as Robert Greene points out, "inspire fear and insecurity" within the master, usually resulting in the banishment, not to mention the death, of the seeming inferior. Knowing this, it is much better for a shrewd power player to make a master feel even more masterful. This is basically what this Law is about.

But we also need to understand that masters are not just individuals or people, per se. Masters also come in the form of groups, and even nations. America is a prime example of a "master nation," because it is the power center of the world, which explains why most less-powerful nations think twice before going against this juggernaut we call the United States. Similarly, the Catholic Church could be considered an example of a master group, due to the massive influence of its Christian doctrine and world power, in general. And powerful master groups also exist in politics—groups that, at the moment, hold more power than Donald Trump. In the power sense, these groups are Trump's "masters."

If we were to ask ourselves, "Well, if Trump isn't the master, then, who is?" the answer to this question would have to be the GOP and its Tea Party, because it would have been nearly impossible for Trump to win the Republican nomination without them. Therefore, knowing this, if Trump really wants to get into the White House as President, the stupidest thing that he could ever do is outshine and refuse to compromise with such groups. Conservative power and influence lie at their feet, and Trump is definitely smart enough to recognize this and see that it would be in his best interest to make these masters feel more masterful than they actually are. And it appears that this is exactly what Trump is doing, and has done. Here is an example.

During the presidential primaries, in order to become the presumptive Republican presidential nominee and make people take him seriously, Trump had to wage political warfare on his Republican opponents. During that time, many spats occurred between Trump and them, and many other powerful Republicans said that they would not even support The Donald. For instance, Bob Dole would not even commit to voting for Trump. Eric Cantor said that a Trump-Clinton matchup was "probably not the best choice for anybody." And Marco Rubio had unleashed an array of sharp attacks upon Trump while running against him. Then, things changed. Unexpectedly, Dole, Cantor and Rubio reversed their stances and publicly *endorsed* Trump! But there is more. *GQ Magazine* released a photo gallery piece entitled "The 50 Most Powerful People in Washington Photos." Among this list of people, guess whose faces popped up: Eric Cantor and Marco Rubio. Other names included Mitch McConnell, Kevin McCarthy, John Boehner and Paul Ryan—all powerful Republicans who are either members of, or have ties to, the GOP and Tea Party. Trump winning over these powerful people was not the result of him outshining them. He did it by making them underestimate him, and by not going too far in displaying his political talents. Case in point: Eric Cantor, in a CNBC interview, admitted that he had underestimated Trump as a presidential candidate, and alluded that Trump had changed the rules of the game.

It is also a well-known fact that Paul Ryan (whose name also appears on the "50 Most Powerful People" list) is one of the most powerful members of the GOP, and the same is true concerning Sarah Palin and the Tea Party. Because Trump could not win the Republican presidential nomination without the GOP and Tea Party, this, in a sense, made Ryan and Palin two of his "masters." Outshining them would have greatly lessened his power, so winning them over was the only alternative. He had already succeeded with Palin, which was no hard feat at all, since she is very vulnerable and susceptible to seduction. So, Ryan became Trump's primary focus concerning this Law. Eventually, as was broadcast all over the world news, Trump won him over.

After the primaries were over and Donald was the last man standing, Ryan said in an interview that he was "just not ready" to back Trump. However, Trump, under the guise of Republican unity, and knowing how passionate Ryan was about party unification, agreed to meet with Ryan. They met, and it was broadcast that other meetings were in the works. But here is what tells us how powerful Trump's strategy was: after the meeting, the two Republicans released a joint statement about how they were committed to working together in order to unify their party, in spite of their differences. Who do you think masterminded that? And Trump went on to speak well of Ryan—he did not go around trying to outshine him publicly. Shortly after, Ryan officially boarded the Trump Train.

As for Sarah Palin being vulnerable and easily seduced, I mean every word of it. Her general psychology and major political loss to Barack Obama in 2008, I believe, is what makes her so susceptible to seduction. In Robert Greene's book, *The Art of Seduction*, there is a section titled "The Seducer's Victims—The 18 Types," and Palin falls *directly* under type five: "The Crushed Star." So that you can see this for yourself, I want you to keep Palin in mind while reading the following excerpt from Greene's book:

The Crushed Star

We all want attention, we all want to shine, but with most of us, these desires are fleeting and easily quieted. The problem with Crushed Stars is that at one point in their lives they did find themselves the center of attention— perhaps they were beautiful, charming and effervescent, perhaps they were athletes, or had some other talent—but those days are gone. They may seem to have accepted this, but the memory of having once shone is hard to get over. In general, the appearance of wanting attention, of trying to stand out, is not seen too kindly in polite society or in the workplace. So, to get along, Crushed Stars learn to tamp down their desires; but failing to get the attention they feel they deserve, they also become resentful. You can recognize Crushed Stars by certain unguarded moments: they suddenly receive some attention in a social setting, and it makes them glow; they mention their glory days, and there is a little glint in the eye; a little wine in the system, and they become effervescent. Seducing this type is simple: just make them the center of attention. When you are with them, act as if they were stars and you were basking in their glow. Get them to talk, particularly about themselves. In social situations, mute your own colors and let them look funny and radiant by comparison. In general, play the Charmer. The reward of seducing Crushed Stars is that you stir up powerful emotions. They will feel intensely grateful to you for letting them shine. To whatever extent they had felt crushed and bottled up, the easing of that pain releases intensity and passion, all directed at you. They will fall madly in love....

See, in 2008, John McCain made Palin the center of attention in politics. She had very big dreams of becoming the first female Republican Vice President of the United States. However, Obama crushed that dream by taking the presidency in a landslide. And many would argue that this created a resentment in her that has lasted to this very day. Then entered Donald Trump, a charming mastermind with the power to make her shine again if he were to win their party's nomination for President. And the fact that she had known him for a while only made the seduction easier. She has been happily "riding" the Trump Train ever since. Simply put, by seduction definition, Palin is a Crushed Star yearning to shine again. And this is why I believe she endorsed Trump—even if she does not know the real reason behind it herself. If you still do not believe me, go to YouTube and watch the full video of Sarah Palin endorsing Donald Trump. Just put "Full Video: Sarah Palin Endorses Donald Trump" into the search bar and click on the CBSN video that has over a million views. Pay attention to how composed Trump is while he is letting her shine, as well as to how *excited* she is to be shining again—seduction at its finest.

Anyway, the point is that Trump is not outshining his masters—he is letting *them* shine. By doing so, he has attained the heights of power, and this is what a true mastermind does.

Law 2
Never Put Too Much Trust in Friends, Learn How to Use Enemies

The main problem with making new friends is that, oftentimes, after you let your guard down and let them in, out of the blue, they tend to start acting shady, seemingly for no reason at all. And the friends that you already have can only be trusted on certain levels. Of course, this is not true regarding *all* friends, but definitely most. If they care about you too much and you have big dreams, big goals, etc., and your plan to accomplish those dreams is a tad bit controversial, they will try their best to talk you out of whatever it is that your gut is telling you to do, claiming that doing so is in your best interest. And, if they are insecure, your big dreams and success will make them jealous, and they will try to sabotage you. They rarely, if ever, tell you what they *really* think about you. But none of this insecure, emotional shit is a factor when you are dealing with enemies on common ground, because both your enemy and you already know how one feels about the other, and your shared goal trumps emotion. You both want the same thing, and if your enemy is a former friend, he or she will have more to prove in order to regain your favor. Therefore, they would do more for you than a typical friend would do and, for that, I say, "Fuck friends." From the strategic perspective, it is much better to use your enemies—something that I believe Donald Trump has done quite well. In fact, it seems as if the closer Trump gets to the White House, the more he is seen with his former foes—and the more they endorse him. Here are some examples.

Many of us remember that unforgettable spat between Donald Trump and American journalist Megyn Kelly during and after the Fox News Republican debate, in which Kelly confronted Trump about his constant stance reversal on several issues. They were at each other's throats in the media for what seemed like forever, and there was no doubt in the public's mind that they were enemies. However, that was before Trump slaughtered all of his competition during the Republican primaries and became the presumptive Republican nominee. A couple months later, Trump shocked the world by appearing in his first extensive interview with Kelly since their squabble at the prior debate—and they got along well. Trump, a man who rarely, if ever, says he is sorry for anything, even apologized to Kelly on live television, admitting that he was sorry for calling her a "bimbo." And, guess what—her ratings went up, resulting in Trump getting a lot of free publicity that cast him in a *positive* light. Now, people are saying that Kelly is a Trump supporter.

Trump also turned to his former political foe, retired neurosurgeon Ben Carson, who ran against him during the primaries, to assist him in his search for a potential Vice President. In fact, at the time of this writing, many of those who ran against Trump during the primaries, or simply doubted and bashed him in the media during that time, are now endorsing him. This includes Wisconsin governor Scott Walker, former Louisiana governor Bobby Jindal, New Hampshire senator Kelly Ayotte and former White House press secretary Ari Fleischer. Though I believe he would never admit it, Trump is using all of this to his advantage. Every former enemy who endorses Trump is doing him a great service because, by supporting him, many of their own supporters begin joining the Trump Crusade. In this way, Trump's enemies are more useful than his friends are. Even Paul Ryan's primary opponent, Paul Nehlen, is endorsing Trump. Here is what he had to say, according to Jim Hoft of TheGatewayPundit.com:

> *If Ryan was even vaguely interested in the will of the people, rather than his own agenda and self-advancement, he'd find a way to work with the choice of the people…This is a classic example of Paul Ryan saying one thing and doing another. He wants us to believe he's the great unifier, but his actions reveal him as the great divider. It isn't the will of the people to engage in secret shenanigans. It isn't the will of the people to parachute in at the eleventh hour a GOP hand-selected candidate that they had nothing to do with selecting. There is already a candidate out there who campaigned, who got voters on board, who won Republican delegates…If Mr. Trump is the nominee, I will support that decision, because it will have been the will of the voters that got him there.*

At the end of the day, the notion of defeating Hillary Clinton is the common ground for Republicans. Michael Dresser, a contact reporter for *The Baltimore Sun*, recently made this clear in an article entitled "Former Gov. Bob Ehrlich, former Kasich backer, endorses Trump to beat Clinton." The article talks about how "Governor Robert L. Ehrlich Jr., a former backer of Ohio Gov. John Kasich, posted a message on Facebook Wednesday night telling Republicans, 'It is time to get our act together' and rally behind Trump to defeat Democrat Hillary Clinton." People who used to be anti-Trump, and many of whom opposed him directly and said nasty things about him both in private and in the media, are coming out of the woodwork to support The Donald. If you doubt that Trump is exercising this Law, you should know that even Trump himself has talked about how he could use his enemies. A *TIME* article by Maya

Rhodan entitled "Donald Trump Would 'Love' to Have Former Rivals in His Cabinet" talks about this. Rhodan points out how Trump talked about uniting the Republican Party, and quoted what he said about his former enemies Marco Rubio, Ben Carson and Chris Christie. Here is what the article says:

> *"Frankly, Marco, I'd love to have involved," Trump said of his former foe. "I can tell you that Ben Carson is a terrific guy. ... Chris Christie is a fantastic guy. Both of them are tremendous people."*

Can you see the strategy now, how Trump plays nice with his foes, because of their usefulness? This is what mastermind strategists do, how they play the game.

Law 3
Conceal Your Intentions

When it comes to Trump's intentions, the truth is that no one really knows what he is up to. The only thing that they can do is speculate, which gives him more power. Because he never reveals his strategy or plan of attack, no one knows how to beat him. And you had better believe that Trump is concealing his intentions on purpose. When people do this, they throw others off their game. And, in order to keep them off, one has to be and remain unpredictable, which Trump is and does quite well. But here is how we know for sure that Trump is employing this strategy: he has told us himself. Most of us were just not paying attention, because we were either distracted by countless other things, or not looking at all of this from the perspective of strategy. But, if you missed what Trump said, just pull up the news article by Eric Levitz entitled "Donald Trump Assures Voters That They'll Never Know What He'll Do as President." Here is what the article says:

> *At a recent rally in New Hampshire, Trump promised his supporters a foreign policy that neither they nor America's enemies could ever anticipate. "I want to be unpredictable," Trump declared. "We want to go in, we don't want them*

*to know what the hell we're doing. We have to go in, and
people love it when I say that."*

Even though Trump was speaking in reference to foreign policy,
his utilization of this third Law is obvious. In the game of power,
concealment of one's intentions just comes with the territory.

Law 4
Always Say Less Than Necessary

Because Trump is so straightforward, he sometimes has a tendency to
utter statements that go on to spark all kinds of controversy. But that
normally happens during trivial matters. When his game face is on, he
says only what *needs* to be said, and that is it. And he does it in a sort
of vague way that keeps people guessing. This is part of the reason why
critics make fun of what seems to be his constant "flip-flopping" on
issues, but it is much deeper than that. And it oftentimes seems as if
Trump is talking too much, but if you analyze what he is saying, you
will notice that he is just repeating the same thing in different ways.
He is saying less, but it *seems* like more. I do not have to go into much
detail about Trump's application of this Law because, if you simply pay
attention to what he is saying when he is talking about virtually anything,
it will become obvious. Just watch him and listen to what he is saying
the next time you see him on television, especially during a speech or
interview, and you will see this for yourself.

Law 5
So Much Depends On Reputation—Guard It with Your Life

Hands down, Trump has a reputation for going after what he wants and
getting it; hitting his enemies back harder after they attack him first; not
taking shit from *anybody*; generally going against the grain and bucking
political correctness; speaking his mind in spite of people's opinions
about what he is saying; and keeping his word. This is why he has been
so successful as a businessman before he even "cannonballed" his way
into politics. He has an image to uphold and will not let anything, or
anybody, mess it up. A recent example of this is his latest threat against
the media, in which he promised to "open up" federal libel laws to make

it easier to sue news outlets like *The Washington Post* and *The New York Times*, to which journalists reacted in horror. But this is just Trump guarding his reputation with his life, because people try to damage it all the time, with journalists and reporters at the top of the list. At the time of this writing, a *New York Times* article entitled "Crossing the Line: How Donald Trump Behaved with Women in Private" is considered by many people an attempt to assassinate Trump's character by pointing out his alleged misconduct with women over decades. So, you had better believe that, if Trump becomes President, even if he cannot create new laws that make it easier to sue news outlets, I believe that he will definitely do his best to make life harder for the journalists and reporters who play dirty games via ink and camera. His hit list is probably 50 times longer than *Nairaland News'* list of Kim Kardashian's sex partners, but how could you blame him? Trump is definitely guarding his reputation with his life.

Politics is truly a dirty game and, when you pop up on the scene winning again and again and again, your biggest haters come out in full force, plotting behind the scenes to knock you clean out of the race. Concerning the misconduct of women, "they" did the same thing to Herman Cain when he was kicking political ass back in 2011. They whipped up a sexual harassment scandal that resulted in him suspending his presidential campaign. Based on my own observation, the average person who followed this in the media back then, but believed he was guilty, now believes he was innocent from the beginning. I have asked so many people what changed their minds, and they have all told me the same thing, essentially: "Because it was a set-up. They knew his 9-9-9 plan was going to work, and he was going to win. So, they had to knock him off." And I agree. In spite of this, both Trump and Cain have been able to uphold their reputations, which they guard with their lives. If you ever become powerful, you had better do the same thing.

Law 6
Court Attention at All Cost

Trump does this *naturally*. Instead of going unnoticed and getting lost in the crowd, he is hovering *above* the crowd, making it virtually impossible for people to *not* notice him. He commands attention, has fantastic stage presence, is literally *made* for TV, and *dominates* the media. This is how masterminds stay relevant. The funniest thing I have ever seen that showed me just how powerful Trump's presence is in the media was a video of a black Muslim immigrant (unaffiliated with Louis Farrakhan and the Nation of Islam) threatening to kill Donald Trump, because of Trump's comments about banning Muslims from entering America. If you have not seen it, please go to YouTube and watch the video entitled "Black Muslim Immigrant Threatens to Kill Donald Trump." In it, this guy is yelling, cussing up a storm, waving knives and calling Donald Trump "pussy," among other things. He is so emotional. I also saw him in another video waving a gun around. He is just like millions of other people across the country, not to mention the world, who actually believe that the Social Matrix is real. They get so caught up into it that they lash out and get themselves into a world of trouble, when all they had to do in the first place was take time out to learn about power and strategy, and pay attention to the social game we call "politics." Those who court attention the most have the power to affect people like this, and such negative reactions only draw more attention to the mastermind, making him or her more famous. Reports have shown that Trump, at this point, has gotten nearly $2 billion in free media attention. Hell, with that said, enough said!

Law 7
Get Others to Do the Work for You, but Always Take the Credit

Quite frankly, if you pay attention, it is easy to see that Trump excels at this. Thomas Jefferson once stated that "Information is the currency of democracy," and if Trump knows nothing else, though he obviously knows a lot, he definitely knows how to access information when needed. And anyone who knows how to access information knows how to access skilled people to do essential work that needs to be done.

For example, it is a well-known fact that Donald Trump is not a veteran speaker or debater, in the traditional political sense. As far as I know, he is not a Toastmaster. And critics talk about this all the time. However, when the time comes for him to speak, he does a good enough job to get his point across, and a superb job making his message resonate with listeners. It would not surprise me if word were to get out that Trump trains inside of simulated debate rooms prior to actually entering debates because, if I were he, even though I am a veteran Toastmasters debater, I would probably do the same thing. I recently read that Trump now has speechwriters and plans to use Teleprompters when times call for such, but most people forget all about Teleprompters while watching most candidates debate, because they are too drawn into the spectacle before them. Thus, they never realize that someone else drafts many of the words coming out of the speakers' mouths, and the speakers themselves get credit for whatever is said.

One could definitely say that Trump pays for a lot of the legwork he gets credit for. But that is just the way the game is played, and why do something yourself that someone else can do for you? I remember a *Daily News* article I read a while back by John Lott Bradley Smith, entitled "Donald Trump's Big Lie About 'Buying' Politicians." It talks about how Trump himself has "bought" politicians. The proof that Trump exercises this seventh Law is found in the fact that he, in so many words, even admitted it himself. The article states:

> *For years, Trump was a major contributor to Democratic campaigns. From 1989 through 2011, Trump gave over $580,000 to Democrats, approximately $85,000 more than he donated to Republicans. He also contributed at least $100,000 to the Clinton Foundation. Since 2012, however, over 99% of his contributions have gone to Republicans.... Trump might have argued his political giving has changed simply because his views on health care, taxes and other issues have grown more conservative. But he has offered quite a different explanation. He says that he has given to politicians not out of conviction, but because then they "do whatever the hell you want them to do."*

As you can see, according to his own words, Trump has an extensive history of giving money to politicians, so that they can do whatever they are told to do. But does this mean that he is "buying" politicians? His comment about Hillary Clinton, found in the same article, answers this question. In fact, let me put it in italicized, boldface type:

> **"With Hillary Clinton, I said, 'Be at my wedding,' and she came to my wedding . . . She had no choice, because I gave."**

The point is that a man like Trump, who has been strategizing for most of his life, would not have gotten where he is today without using the legwork of other people in order to accomplish his goals. And it is he who gets the credit. He even gets tons of kudos for having one of the most historical presidential campaigns ever, when it is really his key staff and advisors putting in the bulk of the work. Only those among us who are soft would state that there is a problem with someone applying this Law. The strong and wise see it a different way. He is the boss, so, he is *supposed* to get the credit. Period.

Law 8
Make Other People Come to You—Use Bait If Necessary

It is hard for me not to laugh while writing about Trump's application of this eighth Law, because all I can think about is how he used it on Ted Cruz so artfully. I know you probably remember that my-wife's-prettier-than-yours meme that Trump tweeted, which got Old Ted all riled up. My god, that was so funny! The meme featured two photos, side-by-side: an apparently ugly-looking one of Heidi Cruz, Ted's wife, and a beautiful one of Melania Trump, Donald's obviously hot flame. The image reads: "No need to 'spill the beans, the images are worth a thousand words.'" Unable to compose himself, Old Ted just lost control and responded to Trump on live television. Here is what he said, among other things:

> *It's not easy to tick me off. I don't get angry often. But you mess with my wife, you mess with my kids, that'll do it every time. Donald, you're a sniveling coward—and leave Heidi alone….*

Ha! Remember that? To me, it actually sounded as if Old Ted had rehearsed that part several times before uttering these words on TV, and I giggle at the random thought of him standing before a mirror during rehearsal, acting it all out and talking to himself, like some cowards do before confronting a bully or feared enemy. I bet Donald was laughing his ass off the whole time while watching this. As for myself, I was literally rolling on the floor laughing, and I tend to go into hysterics if I even *think* about it too long. This was a perfect example of Law 8 in action. Here is what *The 48 Laws of Power* says about Law 8, in summary:

When you force the other person to act, you are the one in control. It is always better to make your opponent come to you, abandoning his own plans in the process. Lure him with fabulous gains—then attack. You hold the cards.

Trump was in control from the beginning, and Cruz did not even see it coming. Had he equipped himself with *The 48 Laws of Power*, and spent his time applying them instead of trying to do what was politically correct, he would have really given Trump a run for his money. But he did not do so, and now he has to take his devastating loss with him to the grave.

Anyway, in another instance, Trump also toyed with Old Cruz's mind by insinuating on Fox News that Cruz's father, Rafael Cruz, was connected to Lee Harvey Oswald—the assassin who, allegedly, murdered President John F. Kennedy. And, then, what happened? As expected, Predictable Ted went berserk! All Trump did was bring up a questionable *National Enquirer* story that claimed Old Rafael was in a photo with the assassin shortly before the murder of the President took place, and that was it. But he knew that this would push Cruz's buttons. In reference to Rafael, here is what Trump said:

I mean, what was he doing? What was he doing with Lee Harvey Oswald shortly before the death, before the shooting? It's horrible.

In a press conference, after emotion had gotten the best of him, Cruz responded:

I'm going to do something I haven't done for the entire campaign: I'm going to tell you what I really think of Donald Trump. This man is a pathological liar. He doesn't know the difference between truth and lie. He lies, practically every word that comes out of his mouth. The man is utterly amoral. Morality does not exist for him.

Cruz saying what he "really" thinks about Donald Trump was proof that his emotions had gotten the best of him, and he cracked beneath the pressure of The Donald, as Trump had already known he would. And his comment about morality not existing for Trump was further proof that he was too weak to play the power game, a game in which morality *has* no power. But, most importantly, to Cruz's supporters, he was God. However, Trump, the proverbial "Devil," as some might call him, made God *bleed*—and then made him cry. And no supposed-to-be God lasts long after his mortality is revealed by other mortals.

Anyway, here is how Trump responded in a comeback:

> *Over the last week, I have watched Lying Ted become more and more unhinged as he is unable to react under the pressure and stress of losing, in all cases by landslides, the last six primary elections. In fact, coming in last place in all but one of them. Today's ridiculous outburst only proves what I have been saying for a long time—that Ted Cruz does not have the temperament to be President of the United States.*

And, then, Trump's son, Trump Jr., hopped into the political octagon via tweet and delivered a superman punch that ended Old Ted, for good. Here is what Trump Junior said:

> *That was an impressive meltdown. Desperate, but impressive. Reminded me of my 3-year-old coming off a sugar high.*

In the end, in addition to him simply not having enough votes to beat The Donald, this is what knocked Old Ted out of the race.

Law 9
Win Through Your Actions, Never Through Argument

To be honest, there really is not much to be said concerning this Law because, though Trump may be privy to arguing at times, his actions always speak louder than his words. While his Republican opponents spent much of their time arguing during the primaries, Trump spent most of his time *winning*. With 17-0, Trump became the last man standing in his party, while his Democratic opponents were playing catch-up. His arguments sparked controversy, but his actions created success. And he demonstrates this on an almost daily basis.

Law 10
Infection: Avoid the Unhappy and Unlucky

As I stated in the Introduction, "masterminds read books about masterminds." Well, this is because, as the old sayings go, "birds of a feather flock together," and "you are what you eat." Successful people in power know and understand that negativity must sometimes be entertained, but misery is to be *avoided* at all cost, because it is contagious. As they say, misery loves company. Therefore, powerful people tend to surround themselves with other like-minded people in the power realm, which is why Trump has an extensive list of happy celebrity friends and acquaintances. He knows that misery is a curse that can destroy an entire empire, so he applies this Law by keeping the right people around him at all times—people who think BIG.

Law 11
Learn to Keep People Dependent on You

When I was growing up, I used to fight a lot, and I remember meeting one guy whom I sort of took under my wing. Where fighting was concerned, what we had most in common was unconventionality. We were both *street* martial artists who despised traditional martial arts, which emphasized humility, because our neighborhoods were *far* from humble. In addition, we were both straight A students, avid readers and thought completely outside of the box. We were bigger than our surroundings, and we knew it. Well, one day, after seeing me knock out an older guy who was thrice my size in a street fight, amazed at how quickly and easily I beat my brutish opponent, in self-defense, my new pupil wanted me to train him in preemptive counterattacks.

So, I did. But I never taught him *everything* I knew, because there was always a possibility that we could someday become enemies, in which case he would try to use my own tactics against me. And I was right. A few months later, after a heated argument, he convinced himself that he was a better fighter than I was, and I ended up kicking his ass, literally. I must admit, he gave me a good fight, even touched me up a little, using a few strategies I had taught him. But he never had a shot at winning, because my skill set was too advanced, and he depended on me for guidance and instruction. To this day, I bet he still has dreams of my knees and elbows flying at him like stealth fighter jets. After this incident, though, in order to prevent anything from being used against me, I vowed to never teach anyone most of what I know.

Lessons like this make it easy to understand this particular power Law because, in an arena of snakes, one of the only ways to avoid being bitten is to keep the snakes dependent upon you. And never teach them your tricks. If no one else understands this, I know Donald Trump does. As a billionaire strategist in a game where money can buy power, Trump applies this law easily. Many of his campaign interns are dependent on him for taking their careers to the next level. Pro-Trump voters are also depending on him, hoping that he will make their lives better if he is elected President. Even a lot of reporters and journalists depend on him to boost their ratings. But one thing Trump does *not* do is reveal his strategies to *any* of these people. Maybe a select few, but that is about it. As long as people are dependent upon him, and he continues to keep them so, he will stay in the game for a long time. Most powerful people like Trump apply this Law naturally.

Law 12
Use Selective Honesty and Generosity to Disarm Your Victim

In our society, the word "victim" has a negative connotation, which implies that someone has been "done" something by someone else. However, as Robert Greene points out in *The Art of Seduction*, in the *game* of power and seduction, people are not victims—they *want* to be seduced. Why do you think they spend so much time opening themselves up to seduction? In the political sphere, on both the Democrat and Republican sides, voters and *potential* voters are paying more attention to this 2016 political dogfight than ever. They want whoever they are supporting to say or do something that they agree with, so that they can feel better. And most of them are just getting off on the thrill of it all, because it is all political entertainment, except to those politicians who take it all too seriously. Point black, they are "buying" what the politicians are "selling," and doing it because they *want* to, on their *own* volition. So, as Greene would probably agree, they are almost always *willing* victims. And Trump is too smart of a power player to not know this.

But let us switch up the terminology for a second. Instead of calling these people "victims," let us simply refer to them as what they are: fans and potential fans. And the best way to win these people over is to seem honest while giving them something they want. In Trump's case, what he is giving them is truth and a dream. People like author Jodi Dean, who understand *real* political strategy, know exactly what I am talking about. Here is an excerpt from an article Dean wrote for *In These Times* magazine, entitled "Donald Trump Is the Most Honest Candidate in American Politics Today: Where Other Candidates Appeal to a Fictitious Unity or Pretense of Moral Integrity, He Displays the Power of Inequality." Dean's work adds weight to what I am saying about Trump exercising this 12th Law of power. Check it out:

> *Donald Trump cuts through the ideological haze of American politics and exposes its underlying truth, the truth of enjoyment. Where other candidates appeal to a fictitious unity or pretense of moral integrity, he displays the power of inequality. Money buys access—why deny it? Money creates opportunity— for those who have it. Money lets those with a lot of it express their basest impulses and desires—there is no need to hide the dark drives when there is none before whom one might feel shame (we might call this the Berlusconi principle). It's the rest of us who bow down.*

> *As Trump makes explicit the power of money in the contemporary US, he facilitates, stimulates, and circulates enjoyment (jouissance). Trump openly expresses the racism, sexism, contempt, and superiority that codes of civility and political correctness insist be repressed. This expression demonstrates the truth of economic inequality: civility is for the middle class, a normative container for the rage of the dispossessed and the contempt of the dispossessors. The .1 % need not pretend to care.*

> *The freedom from civility, the privilege of enjoying superiority, incites different responses, all of which enable people to enjoy—get off on—this political round.*

By focusing on truths that most of us already know but are too afraid to talk about, Trump has placed himself upon a pedestal of honesty in the public eye. The more this honesty is resisted based on the notion of political correctness, the more people gravitate toward Trump, the truth teller. And Trump's generosity comes in the form of giving his supporters a platform that allows them to speak what they truly *feel*, many of them for the first time in a long time, if ever. This honesty and generosity disarms them, making it easier for the Trump campaign to mobilize them like never before in its quest for presidential deadlock.

Law 13
When Asking for Help, Appeal to People's Self-Interest, Never to Their Mercy or Gratitude

When you want people to help you, you have to remember that, because most people have their own personal shit going on, they are only going to help you if you can help *them*. That is just common sense. Trump's political success is shocking many people, and a lot of them want to know what his secret formula for success is. All the time, people ask me, "Why are so many people supporting Trump?" One of the things I tell them is this: "They are supporting him because they see something that can be gained for themselves." They want jobs, and he is an expert job creator. He speaks his mind and does not care what other people think about him, and supporting him gives them an opportunity to do what they have been wanting to do for a long time: say what is really on their minds. They are fed up with the way the Democrats have been handling things during their last two terms in office, and they can get credit for helping Trump turn things around. The list goes on. Trump's base primarily consists of the dissatisfied among us, and we know this. So, when a hugely famous, bold, likeable, wealthy man announces his official run for president and tells these dissatisfied people, "We are going to make America great again," they feel a connection to him. They believe that, in order to get what they truly want out of life, America has to become great again, because a great nation provides great opportunity to its people. This campaign slogan, "Make America Great Again," is the same one used by Ronald Reagan back in 1980, but it still appeals to people's self-interest. And Trump knows this, though he probably would never admit it, and he is not supposed to. A lot of these politicians are schmucks with their heads stuck so far up their asses that they cannot see Trump's shrewdness for what it is, and this is what gives him the advantage.

Law 14
Pose as a Friend, Work as a Spy

There has been much talk over the years about Donald Trump's "cozy relationship" with the tabloids, and I have seen reports claiming that he is seriously connected with the folks at *The National Enquirer*. Average people believe that the tabloids are "bad," because all they seem to do is report gossip. But people who think bigger than average and understand the game of power have a different perspective. They know that, as mentioned earlier, a person's reputation is everything, and that opening up holes in an enemy's reputation can help assure triumph on the battlefield. Thus, the use of tabloids for this purpose is a beneficial strategy. And BIG thinkers also know that gossip sparks controversy—and controversy sells. If Trump is really connected to the tabloids, which I believe he is, then this is a good thing, not a bad one, because it allows him to use popular gossip as a weapon to defeat opponents who will not allow themselves to play as "dirty" as he is playing. In *real* warfare, there are no goddamn rules! If you are not going to go all out, as necessity requires, in order to win, you might as well not even fight at all. And this is something that a lot of these New Age politicians just do not understand.

In *The Art of War*, Sun Tzu says:

> *If you know the enemy and know yourself, you need not fear the result of a hundred battles. If you know yourself but not the enemy, for every victory gained you will also suffer a defeat. If you know neither the enemy nor yourself, you will succumb in every battle.*

See, Trump already knows himself. And he definitely knows his enemies, how to make them tick, just as he did with Ted Cruz and virtually all of his other opponents. This is why he keeps winning so much. However, oftentimes, his enemies know neither themselves nor their enemy, and this is why they lose. Information about a rival is critical on the battlefield, and being connected to the tabloids, who are connected to the paparazzi (spies with cameras), makes information acquisition extremely easy. Moreover, Trump spends a lot of time on social media, Twitter to be specific, which means that he acquires some of his information on the Internet. In fact, on NBC's "Meet The Press," he once told moderator Chuck Todd, "All I know is what's on the Internet." So, we know he searches the Web. By doing so, in addition to having information provided to him via his advisors and tabloid connections, he can also play the spy himself by simply going online and pulling up information that can be used to his advantage against his rivals. Masterminds understand masterminds, so I know that a man like Trump, who has been playing the power game for *decades*, can read people easily. Simply going online and watching his rivals in real-time videos can take him into a rival's psychology and foster intimate understanding, making it easier to manipulate a foe at will. Eventually, all great strategists reach this advanced level of discernment, and Trump is already there. He applies this Law easily.

Law 15
Crush Your Enemy Totally

This Law is Donald Trump all the way, and there is a lot of proof out there revealing his application of it. It is widely known that, when you mess with The Donald, you mess with a Leviathan. He is a giant at heart, and this is why so many people are afraid of him. They do not want to feel his wrath.

An example of this is what happened when Marco Rubio took Trump's bait while battling him during the primaries. Rubio tried to get personal and ended up getting his ass kicked, and his balls handed to him on a bloody platter of shame. Reporter Jake Flanagin wrote about this in a Quartz.com article entitled "Watch: Marco Rubio Looks Like a Beaten Man as He Apologizes for His anti-Trump Insults." If you missed this in the media, here is some of what Flanagin reported:

Marco Rubio is losing, and losing badly. The Florida senator is trailing Republican frontrunner Donald Trump by as many as 20 points in his home state—a primary that is absolutely crucial to the survival of Rubio's campaign.

This might be why the senator's latest sit-down with Fox News in Miami last night (March 9) sounded so much like a post-mortem for a failed campaign. He told Megyn Kelly he regretted getting personal in his attacks on Donald Trump—an abrupt turn toward insult comedy that appears to have totally backfired, decimating Rubio's support while strengthening the New York billionaire.

I actually watched the news clips myself, and I remember seeing Rubio, during his apology, talk about how his children were embarrassed and "he would never do it again." He was not strong enough to win against Trump, his campaign failed miserably and his plan backfired—all because he took the bait and messed with The Donald, who crushed him totally during the primaries. And Trump himself has even declared in the media that his favorite Bible verse is the one referring to "an eye for an eye." Knowing this, it is obvious that, when in battle, Trump can be expected to crush his enemies totally. He definitely applies this Law.

Law 16
Use Absence to Increase Respect and Honor

Remember when Barack Obama became President back in 2008? This was one of the most historic events in American history, and Obama was the talk of the world for many years to come. Though he did a decent job in his first two primary debates, it was not until the third one, where he ripped Mitt Romney to pieces, that most of America started to accept him as a political heavyweight who could actually be President. During his first term, every move he made was scrutinized heavily, as people wanted to see if he would stick to the promises he made during campaign season. He made good on most of those promises, and was all over the news. It was Obama this, Obama that. And this carried him into his second term. But, eventually, the more he was seen, the more people started taking him for granted. Now, to many of the same people who helped him get elected, both times, Obama is perceived as a common politician. They respect and honor him less and less, and the main reason for this is that he has never really been able to take a break from the public. He has never been missed. Since hitting the scene, he has never left. And what people constantly see all the time eventually becomes boring.

Now, as for Trump, candidly speaking, he was the *shit* during the 1980s. The real estate and other deals that he was making made him the talk of the big business community *and* the world, and he was at the top of his game, with a spot on the Forbes Billionaires list—one of the richest men in the world. It was during this time that his book, *The Art of the Deal*, was published to major success, topping the *New York Times* Bestseller list, and holding a position on it for 51 weeks, straight. Then, the 1990s came, and with it, financial difficulty. In 1990, Trump slid off the Forbes list. As the years went on, bankruptcy threatened his empire, and many people thought that he would soon be gone, for good. However, he was hell-bent on keeping his empire intact, so he took a step back and stepped up his game. He was still in the media here and there, but not in dominant fashion as he was during the 1980s. His business dominance took a hiatus, and those who still believed in him were dying to see him make a major comeback. Then, in 1997, he made his way back onto the Forbes list, his financial problems started fading away and he took his brand to an entirely new level. His biggest comeback of all was his earth-shattering splash into politics in 2015, when he announced that he was running for President of the United States, and he single-handedly slaughtered his competition, becoming the presumptive Republican nominee. By taking a break to get his empire straight in the '90s, Trump, unlike Obama, avoided the rut of commonality resulting from overexposure. Due to his absence, people's respect and honor for him increased tenfold. Now, his overall value is at an all-time high. This is typical Law 16.

Law 17
Keep Others in Suspended Terror: Cultivate and Air of Unpredictability

In life in general, being predictable is the worst thing that you can ever be, because it gives other people room to maneuver against you in ways that you cannot foresee. If an opponent knows your patterns, he can predict and even dictate your moves, to your disadvantage. In the game of power, predictable people *always* lose. But, Trump, for the most part, has always been an enigma, and he is no different now. Only *masterminds* understand his strategy, but everyone else is still trying to figure him out. They never will, though, because Trump is being unpredictable on purpose. He has even mentioned this publicly, yet his opponents are still trying to figure him out. The point is that Trump is actively applying this Law, and it not only throws his enemies off balance, but also intimidates the hell out of a lot of them. In case you doubt what I am saying about Trump's implementation of this Law, here is the proof.

Remember the article I mentioned earlier entitled "Donald Trump Assures Voters That They'll Never Know What He'll Do as President"? Well, in this article, here is what Trump is quoted as saying to Bill O'Reilly on *The O'Reilly Factor*:

> *Bill, I'm gonna do what's right. I want to be unpredictable…*
> *The voters want unpredictability.*

He is also quoted in the article as saying:

> *We want to go in; we don't want them to know what the*
> *hell we're doing. We have to go in, and people love it when*
> *I say that.*

The topics on which Trump was speaking are not important. His *mindset* is. He is *deliberately* unpredictable, putting Law 17 into action.

Law 18
Do Not Build Fortresses to Protect
Yourself—Isolation Is Dangerous

Isolation is dangerous because it exposes people to threats. If an enemy is a sitting duck, he is an easy win. But Trump is always on the move, going where The People are, researching rivals on the Internet and "keeping his ear to the streets," so to speak. On top of that, because of who he is, in general, and how much power he has, people just *bring* information to him. Therefore, he is *always* on top of things, and this puts him many steps ahead of his competition. While isolating themselves by roaming in the same political circles that they have been roaming in forever, they limit themselves to selective information gathering and place themselves in the crosshairs of a powerful enemy. But Trump never makes this mistake—he remains focused even when it appears that he is isolated.

Law 19
Know Who You're Dealing with—Do Not Offend the Wrong Person

The reason that Trump has yet to be defeated is that he studies his enemies and, upon discovering their weaknesses, he defeats them by hitting them hard wherever they cannot stand being hit. To some people, it may seem as if Trump is the troublemaker on the battlefield, but this is not true at all, because he is more of a finisher than a starter. Yes, he will definitely throw some bait out there to see who bites, but that is just a strategy he has to use when it is understood that enemies will do the same to him in battle. Therefore, the bait thing is nothing more than preemptive self- defense. Remember, Trump is an "eye for an eye" kind of guy. If you throw a rock at him, he will throw a million boulders back until 500,000 of them hit you. However, when it comes to offending people, it is obvious that he picks his battles carefully, because he has never been seriously defeated by anybody or wiped off the map. Therefore, obviously, he knows exactly who he is dealing with. He is too much of a political Floyd Mayweather *not* to know.

Law 20
Do Not Commit to Anyone

The only person that Trump is truly committed to is himself, and he has a right to be, because the only person he knows that he can trust one hundred percent, on any level, is himself. And I say this while taking family, marriage and friendship out of the equation. When it comes to taking sides or fighting for a cause, committing to anything or anyone other than oneself only limits one's independence. I just finished watching the History Channel documentary, *The Making of Trump,* on DVD, and I remember some of the folks on it talking about how Trump is able to appeal to the dissatisfied voters on both the Democratic and Republican sides. This is so true. When he flirted with the presidency in the past, it seemed as if he was just testing the waters, and doing it in a way that would make him beholden to neither the Democratic nor Republican Party. I believe that, in regard to his current political endeavor, as mentioned on the DVD, Trump knows that it is virtually impossible to become President without running as a Democrat or Republican, and this is why he is running as a Republican—when he is really an Independent at heart. This would explain why he is not only self-funding his own campaign but also at odds with so many Republicans. His mindset is not confined to the ideology of any particular party—it dwells in the realm of *reality*. And this is why people from both parties are gravitating toward him in droves. Self-commitment does not make him selfish. It makes him *smart*. When you commit, you lose a big part of yourself out of obligation to whatever side or cause you have chosen, and your strategy would have to be confined to the rules of that particular side. But Trump thinks BIGGER when it comes to commitment in the game of power. You should, too!

Laws 21-30
Play a Sucker to Catch a Sucker—Seem Dumber Than Your Mark

Trump is much smarter than he looks, and there are many people who can vouch for this, one of whom is former New York City mayor, Rudy Giuliani. In an interview with *The Washington Post* earlier this year, Giuliani said of Trump:

> *You know, he's very good. It's clear that he has an exceptionally good understanding of how the economy affects our foreign policy. He understands what's happening with China, how they could stop North Korea in a heartbeat. This idea that he's only familiar with slogans, it's not accurate at all.*

David Martosko, a political editor for Dailymail.com, mentions this in an article of his entitled "Rudy Giuliani Says Trump Is Smarter than He Looks, as The Donald Consults with Former NYC Mayor and Other 'Kitchen Cabinet' Advisers." People who really know Trump know that he is a mastermind who can strategically play dumb when he wants to. He did it when he played dumb during the whole KKK and David Duke endorsement controversy. In an interview with Jake Tapper on CNN's State of the Union, here is what The Donald said:

> *Well, just so you understand, I don't know anything about David Duke, OK? I don't even know anything about what you're talking about with white supremacy or white supremacists. Did he endorse me, or what's going on? I know nothing about David Duke. I know nothing about white supremacists.*

But, back in 2000, here is what he said on World News Now:

> *As you know, the Reform Party has got some pretty big problems, not the least of which is Pat Buchanan, David Duke, Fulani, and it's a problem.*

He also wrote the following in the *New York Times*:

> *Although I am totally comfortable with the people in the New York Independence Party, I leave the Reform Party to David Duke, Pat Buchanan and Lenora Fulani. That is not company I wish to keep.*

So, Trump *definitely* knows who David Duke is, and has known for quite a while. However, this does not make Trump a racist. Whatever his motive was for playing dumb, only *he* knows. But the point is that he exercised this Law by playing dumb about it, and it eventually blew over. I honestly believe that the liberal media blew up this whole David Duke thing to prevent African Americans from voting for The Donald, knowing that, if he were to ever reach this demographic on a decent scale, he would literally *steal* the presidency. As an African American myself, I can attest to this because, although many older people in my demographic have been systematically conditioned to be anti-conservative, I know for a fact that there are still countless blacks who can see through Hillary Clinton's bullshit. They would definitely vote for Trump if his message were to reach and resonate with them in the right way. The biggest hurdle is just breaking through the democratic conditioning.

Herman Cain once said the following:

> *African-Americans have been brainwashed into not being open-minded, not even considering a conservative point of view. I have received some of that same vitriol simply because I am running for the Republican nomination as a conservative. So, it's just brainwashing and people not being open-minded, pure and simple.*

Cain was right, and it is all about delivering the Trump message the *right* way, something that people like Al Sharpton and NewsOne's Roland Martin could *never* do, due to in-box, race card-related thinking. In addition, to be honest, I believe that this is an area in which I could *definitely* be beneficial to Trump's campaign. If Trump were to contact me today or tomorrow, saying, "Hey, Niccolò. We're ready to start targeting the African American demographic," as long as the resources are there to help me pull it off, I'd be down for it to the end, because I know exactly where to go and who to talk to get votes. People respect me. They know that I am real, will tell them the truth and take their messages *directly* to the Trump campaign, without modification. Such is the benefit of thinking outside of the box.

Use the Surrender Tactic: Transform Weakness into Power

When Trump flirted with the presidency a while back and dropped out of the race, a lot of politicians back then thought he was a joke, believing that he was not only ill-equipped to succeed politically, but also too weak to fight in general. By dropping out, they thought he was surrendering for good. However, some people out there will tell you that Trump had plans to do what he is doing now all along, and his appearance of surrender was nothing more than a strategy used to make his opponents underestimate him when he truly decided to take the political plunge. And this is exactly what they did when he officially hit the political scene: underestimated him. This gave him an advantage like no other. By using the surrender tactic and biding his time, then later coming back and slaughtering his enemies, he transformed weakness into power.

Concentrate Your Forces

Basically, this Law is about staying focused on your goal and knowing what avenue to take in order to get to power the best way, and keep you there. Where Trump is concerned, he knew that, with all of the public dissatisfaction with the Obama administration, running for President as a Democrat would not have elevated him high enough. So, the only alternative was running as a Republican. And it worked. His "Make America Great Again" movement is a force to be reckoned with, with members of all calibers moving it forward like a tank. And Trump and his squad are going for the gusto like hungry lions during a drought. At the moment, the Democrats are not as focused, and this is why Trump is so much of a threat to them. He and his forces are concentrated and ready to roll until the wheels fall off.

Play the Perfect Courtier

As it regards power and seduction, a courtier is a person who uses flattery, charm, etc., to get what he or she wants. Those who do not understand the courtier strategy say that it is nothing more than ass kissing, but they are sadly mistaken. Robert Greene puts it this way:

> *The perfect courtier thrives in a world where everything revolves around power and political dexterity. He has mastered the art of indirection; he flatters, yields to superiors, and asserts power over others in the most oblique and graceful manner. Learn and apply the laws of courtiership and there will be no limit to how far you can rise in the court.*

True courtiers tend to be subtle, master manipulators who oftentimes become more powerful than the people they aim to seduce, and Trump has this skill down pat. To be a master manipulator is not a bad thing, I must add, because if you do not learn how to manipulate others, they will surely end up manipulating you. To manipulate is to influence, and who among us has never influenced someone to do something that we wanted he or she to do? Therefore, manipulation is a *good* thing, especially when in pursuit of a major goal, and only an insecure person who has never felt manipulatively victimized by something or someone would tell you something different.

One article that talks about Trump's master manipulation skills is "Donald Trump, Master Manipulator," which Jacob Franklin wrote for *The Daily Caller*. Here is some of what Franklin pointed out:

> *Donald Trump is a master manipulator. Trump manipulates the GOP, the Democrats, and the entire media with what appears to be incredible ease. But the manipulation by itself isn't what is impressive. It is how masterful he is at doing it on several fronts...The most impressive manipulation by Trump is that of the media, which is one of the highest hurdles that the GOP faces every hour of every day. Not only does Trump control the entire media cycle by sucking the air out the entire media bubble, but Trump also has nearly the entire media flat-footed, if not completely on their heels. This is a media that is on a perpetual cycle of search and destroy missions against any conservative. Trump has this same media flat-out scared to ask tough questions or smear him as they would others in the GOP.*

Trump has strategically manipulated his way to the top, and the fact that he is still winning means that he will not stop anytime soon. He is not supposed to. Out of respect for him in regard to his shrewd application of this particular strategy, I will not go into detail about any of the *people* he has manipulated, because that is for you to figure out as you pay attention to him. If you do so with an open mind, it will be hard for you *not* to respect him.

Re-Create Yourself

It has been said that Donald trump is the P.T. Barnum of the modern age and, to this, even Trump himself agrees. Wikipedia describes Phineas Taylor "P.T." Barnum as "an American showman and businessman remembered for promoting celebrated hoaxes and for founding the Barnum & Bailey Circus." Barnum was a master at advertising and promotion, and Robert Greene even talks about some of his strategies in

The 48 Laws of Power. After being compared to Barnum, Trump said on "Meet The Press": "We need P.T. Barnum, a little bit, because we have to build up the image of our country." Like Barnum re-created himself, so did Trump. And this is one of the reasons that he is on top.

Because of his success with real estate deals, people were trying to paint him as someone who was only skilled at property acquisition, and that is it. They wanted to control his image, but eventually failed. Trump went on to become a successful author, celebrity TV star, branding expert and now master political strategist. He constantly commands attention and does it on purpose, so no one will ever forget him—ever.

Keep Your Hands Clean

Throughout his career, Trump has been caught up in countless controversies. But here is the interesting thing: he *always* escapes. Why? Because he keeps his hands clean. I remember reading an article in *The Atlantic* titled "The Many Scandals of Donald Trump: A Cheat Sheet." It talks about some of the main scandals that Trump was embroiled in, which include but are not limited to alleged sexual misbehavior toward women, racial housing discrimination, alleged mafia ties, tenant intimidation on one of his properties, four bankruptcies, the hiring of undocumented Polish workers, the breaking of casino rules, antitrust violations, condo hotel shenanigans and alleged marital rape. Through it all, Trump has been sued countless times, is said to have been named in at least 169 federal lawsuits and has made a number of settlements—but has never been seriously penalized or convicted of a crime. When you really think about it, especially when you see stuff like Bill Cosby's scandal on television, it makes you wonder how, if Trump has ever been guilty of any of this stuff, he has been able to get away with it for so long. Only Trump himself knows what really happened, but the world of power is a place where dirty deeds have to be done because, when you are rich and on top, haters come out of the woodwork trying to slaughter you and take everything you have. That is reality. So, if he has ever played dirty, I do not even blame him. In fact, I respect the *hell* out of him for "keeping his hands clean" all this time. My personal opinion is that no person on the face of this planet as wealthy and powerful as Trump is can build an empire and sustain it without having to play dirty behind the scenes and use scapegoats every now and then, while disguising his or her involvement, in order to appear spotless in the public eye. This is just the way life goes. I believe Trump is so skilled at keeping his hands clean that playing dirty behind the scenes, and getting caught, will *never* be a problem for him. He is too shrewd for that, whether people like it or not.

Play on People's Need to Believe to Create a Cultlike Following

Everyone believes in *something*, and this even includes atheists. In fact, I do not know anyone who does not believe in anything. The closest that most people come to not believing in something is becoming fed up with something they once believed in to the point that they just do not want to deal with it anymore. We see this a lot concerning matters of state and religion. Today, a lot of Democrats and Republicans are leaving their parties and becoming Independents, and a lot of Independents and other people who were never really into voting at all are beginning to join the Democratic and Republican parties. However, a great number of people on all sides are simply fed up with the way that the Obama administration is running the country, and they want a new leader to believe in, which is where Trump comes in. I have already mentioned how his "Make America Great Again" slogan appeals to such people, but there is a much deeper reason that explains why so many of Trump's followers are so radical.

I have read reports claiming that Trump's supporters are just inherently angry radicals harboring vendettas against "The Establishment," but this claim is ridiculous because, if such were true, way before Trump even hit the political scene, they would have already been organizing radically violent protests on their own, striking back at the "system" independently, because this is what *true* radicals do. In truth, from my perspective, the radicalism of Trump's supporters has more to do with shrewd campaign strategy that targets these people's emotions. Even if this were true, it would not be a bad thing, because a movement can only be successful when there is a lot of emotion involved. Hell with what politicians are saying about morality and political correctness. We are humans who think and feel. When our thoughts are filled with truth, and we know that something is wrong, frankly, this causes us to feel fucked up inside, and we tend to express how we feel through what? Thought and emotion. The Trump campaign emphasizes truths that many of us have been denying for too long. Trumpians know and understand this. If this makes them a cult, then so be it. This cult is awakening America!

In *The 48 Laws of Power*, Robert Greene says that, in order to create a cult, one has to do the following:

1. Attract attention, not through action, but through words that are vague and simple.
2. Emphasize the visual and the sensual over the intellectual.
3. Borrow the forms of organized religion to structure the group.
4. Disguise your source of income.
5. Set up an us-versus-them dynamic.

Trump and his campaign adheres to all five of the above. The Trump Train's official infancy began when Donald announced in 2015 that he was officially running for President. There were no outrageous actions involved—just one simple speech that drew everyone's attention. Here are the parts of the speech that gave birth to the beginning of a remarkable movement:

> *So, ladies and gentlemen, I am officially running for president of the United States, and we are going to make our country great again... Sadly, the American dream is dead. But if I get elected president, I will bring it back bigger and better and stronger than ever before.*

The "we" was a call to politically dissatisfied Americans. "Make America great again" insinuated that America is no longer great anymore. The part about the American dream being dead made people question their futures, wondering if they would ever have what virtually all Americans want: the American Dream. And the part about bringing the dream back "bigger and better and stronger than ever" made people imagine a new, *thriving* America that they would want to be a part of. Simple, yet powerful. Even a *child* could understand Trump's language.

When speaking, Trump is really good at creating mental pictures with his words. For example, when he calls Hillary Clinton "Crooked Hillary," a mental image of a criminal or shady character pops up in people's minds. When he referred to Marco Rubio as "Little Rubio," a mental image of someone small and unimportant popped up in people's minds, subconsciously. And his "Lyin' Ted" designation in regard to Ted Cruz conjured up in people's minds an image of an untrustworthy person. And this shit actually worked!

The religious aspect of it all comes in the form of duties performed by Trumpians. One duty is the spreading of news about Trump and his campaign, and another is the attending of Trump rallies. These duties can also be considered "rituals." Christians "spread the news or gospel" about Christ, and they also "attend" church. Similarly, many of Trump's followers have his books, especially *The Art of the Deal*, which many people consider a sort of business bible. See the correlation yet? Many people would probably argue that Trump's delay in releasing his annual tax return fulfills the concealment of income aspect, and the whole us-versus-them thing is simply the battle between Republicans and Democrats. As you can see, all of the elements of a cult are here. You just need to remember that creating a cult to gain power and engender change is not a bad thing. Besides, if you are religious, then, you should know that all of the world's major religions started out as cults.

Enter Action with Boldness

Where Trump is concerned, this is a no-brainer. He is bold as hell, everybody knows it, and his opponents cannot do anything about it. It is just who he is as a person, which makes this Law much easier for him to apply as a strategist. He tells it like it is, goes against the grain and hits his enemies hard when necessity requires. If he makes a mistake, he continues on with more audacity and people just leave him alone, knowing that there is, at the moment, nothing that they can do to stop him or bring him down to their level. In fact, I believe that Trump actually applies this Law more frequently and skillful than any of the others.

Plan All the Way to the End

Only ignorant people who have not been paying attention to Donald Trump maintain the belief that his decision to run for president this time around was based on nothing more than whimsical contemplation. The truth is that Trump seems to have been planning this for years, all while biding his time, waiting on the right moment. It is already a generally known fact that he has tested the presidential waters on occasion years ago. But there is more to the story. Earlier this year, The Wall Street Journal published an article by Heather Haddon entitled "Donald Trump's Presidential Run Was Long in the Making," and in this article, Haddon reveals how Trump has been planning his current campaign for years. Here is an excerpt from her article, so that you can see exactly what I am talking about. I want you to read it for yourself.

> *Donald Trump and a small team of confidants began planning his White House bid just weeks after Mitt Romney's 2012 loss to President Barack Obama…The businessman trademarked his "Make America Great Again" slogan in November 2012, according to federal records. He spoke about the dangers of illegal immigration at the Conservative Action Political Conference in 2013, and campaigned in 2014 for Republican Rep. Steve King in Iowa, home of the first contest in the presidential nomination process.…Establishment Republicans have watched the rise of Mr. Trump's presidential bid this year with shock. And yet, Mr. Trump has been telegraphing his presidential ambitions for decades, including when the ever-confident businessman told Oprah Winfrey in 1988 that he would probably win the presidency if he ever competed for it. "I don't think people realized he has always had presidential aspirations," said Sam Nunberg, a Republican strategist who advised Mr. Trump from 2013 until last August. "He knows the voters he attracts. He knew it from the beginning."*

See, Trump is no fool, and the reason that he has a pretty good shot at winning the presidential election is that he strategically planned how he would do it, and laid the foundation for his success, long before he even took the plunge. Back then, while his future political opponents were bullshitting with politics, forgetting all about strategy, Trump was plotting his rise to the top—and now it seems as if he is almost there. All because he was planning all the way to the end.

Make Your Accomplishments Seem Effortless

If you think about it, Trump never really talks about, from the strategic perspective, how hard he had to work in order to pull off what some consider the most successful Republican presidential campaign in modern American politics. This is why most people, in spite of having a lot of this information readily available via the Internet, are still unaware of his decades-old master plan. And the reason he does not spill the beans is that doing so could cause his enemies to prepare a defense and use this same information against him in their efforts to sabotage his success. And the key benefit of not revealing his master plan is that it makes all of his accomplishments seem effortless, as if he is favored by the gods. Most people do not have the patience and temperament to keep their mouths shut, because they want the world to know how shrewd they are. And people like this almost always fail. As long as Trump continues to conceal his strategy, it will seem as if all of his accomplishments were executed with ease.

Laws 31-40
Control the Options: Get Others to Play with the Cards You Deal

Trump has been controlling the game from the beginning. Instead of playing by standard political rules, he flipped the script and made all of his opponents play by his own set of rules, which were and are the sheer opposite of what they have confined themselves to. Nancy Benac from The Associated Press recently talked about this in her article, "Donald Trump Broke These 12 Rules of Modern Politics, and Won Anyway." So, what are the "12 Rules"? According to Benac, in so many words, they are:

1. Use Political Correctness When Speaking
2. Use Traditional Fundraising for Your Campaign
3. Use Surveys to Conduct Poll Testing
4. Be Consistent at All Times
5. Use Five-Point Policy Plans
6. Refrain from Using Vulgarity During Speeches
7. Rely On Super PACs
8. Avoid Appearing Monetarily Greedy
9. Do Not Insult People

10. Do Not Pick Fights
11. Be "Presidential"
12. Stay Groomed

As we have seen, Trump has broken *all* of these rules. He says whatever he wants to and disdains political correctness. He is funding is campaign in his own way. He does not have a pollster. He flip-flops on issues instead of being consistent. He does not use traditional five-point plans. He has a potty mouth. He disses super PACs. He admits to being greedy. He speaks truths that some people take as insults. He fights with opponents when he has a reason to. He refuses to be "presidential" until the time is right, and he keeps his hair all over the place! Moreover, every time his opponents come out of their comfort zone and try to do what he does to fight him back, they lose, oftentimes miserably. When it seems as if Trump's opponents are winning, the result of this is normally what Trump wanted to happen anyway. He has his enemies adopting his strategies and, as long as they continue to do so, Trump will be controlling the cards.

Play to People's Fantasies

Even though Trump speaks the truth a lot of the time, he also plays to people's fantasies on occasion. And how does he do it? By simply telling them whatever it is that they want to hear. Let me give you an example. Trump knows that a lot of American citizens are tired of businesses taking the cheap way out and hiring undocumented Hispanics to do jobs that were traditionally theirs. He also knows that citizens are concerned about the alleged illegal drug epidemic, and crime rate increases, said to be fueled by the flood of illegal immigrants from Mexico and some of its surrounding countries. So, what does he say? That he will build a border wall to keep undocumented Mexicans and other Hispanics out of the United States. And the crowd goes wild. He knows that many working- and middle-class Americans are tired of seeing American companies send jobs overseas to China, not to mention all of the other countries. So, what else does he say? That he will bring back jobs from China and elsewhere. The crowd goes wild again. And he knows that, after 9/11, many Americans hate terrorism, believe that ISIS is a serious threat to national security and, as a consequence, generally regard Muslims with suspicion. So, he says that he will "bomb the shit out of ISIS and ban all or most overseas Muslims from entering the United States." The crowd screams! Trump caters to the fantasies of the majority, and they flock to him like loyal cattle. This is where a lot of his power comes from in regard to his supporters. If you really want to see just how shrewd Trump is at playing to the fantasies of the masses, you should read Jenna Johnson's article in *The Washington Post*, entitled "Here Are 76 of Donald Trump's Many Campaign Promises." After reading it, there should be no doubt in your mind that Trump is a master at tapping into the fantasies of the masses.

Discover Each Man's Thumbscrew

This is yet another Law at which trump excels. A man's thumbscrew is a man's weakness, which can be used by another against him to his disadvantage. Trump has a knack for discovering an opponent's weakness before he strikes, and this is how he got rid of Ted Cruz by making him overreact to the point of appearing extremely emotional and weak. But Trump is so good at this that, according to some of the reports that I have read, he can discover a *country's* weaknesses and use it against its leaders to get what he wants. Just google "Donald Trump accused of blackmailing Scotland," and you will see what I am talking about. I also remember reading a report about how Trump allegedly has a "blackmail file" on Fox News' Roger Ailes. If this is true, it shows you just how far Trump is willing to go to beat his opponents. If he has the balls to compile troubling information that could be devastating to the world's most powerful news corporation, and attempt blackmail on one of the world's most powerful countries, just imagine how easy it would be for him to do the same to one of his enemies. I honestly believe that Trump simply has a natural ability to discover thumbscrews, as many of his defeated opponents and enemies can affirm.

Be Royal in Your Own Fashion: Act Like a King to Be Treated Like One

Though some people may disagree, in spite of all the controversy surrounding Trump, he definitely conducts himself like a king. Like all kings, he is, unquestionably, far from common and makes himself seem *destined* to wear a crown. On top of the fact that he is a billionaire with an extravagant lifestyle, who acquired his fortune like a king, what really makes him kingly is the way that he strategizes and runs his empire with an iron fist. People can say what they want to say about him, but his track record of innovation and extraordinary success speaks for itself. From the beginning, he believed that he was destined for great things, and he has accomplished most of those things. And he is still at it, his supreme confidence radiating outward for all to see, and this is what mainly resonates with The People. Simply put, he is acting like a king and, when November comes, if he officially wins the election, numerous people who doubted him will *see* him as one, and this will confirm his application of Law 34.

Master the Art of Timing

Haste is not a Trump trait at all and, as aforementioned, we have seen this time and time again during his presidential flirtation days. All signs point to him planning his rise for decades, and waiting for the perfect, most opportune time, to execute a masterful strategy that would confound the world and put him directly in the White House—or as close to it as possible. And he is making history doing this right now. Why? Because timing was everything. He could not have done this to any major success back in the 80s, 90s and early 2000s, because the collective societal mindset in America would not have been open to his radical way of thinking, and this would have gotten him not only ousted from the Republican Party, but most likely killed also. Back then, the political establishment took politics a lot more seriously, and The People were not as freethinking and open-minded as they are now. But, since then, the Establishment has dropped the ball, and The People are ready for a radical leader who will take this country to the next level. In fact, the shortcomings of the political establishment itself are what opened the door for a Donald-Trump-For-President campaign. Now, they just have to deal with it. When the time was not yet ripe, Donald stood back, patiently. And, then, the moment the time came, he struck *fiercely*—pure genius.

Disdain Things You Cannot Have: Ignoring Them Is the Best Revenge

As Robert Greene points out in reference to this Law, "what you do not react to cannot drag you down in a futile engagement. Your pride is not involved. The best lesson you can teach an irritating gnat is to consign it to oblivion by ignoring it." When there is something you absolutely cannot have at the moment, such as a certain revenge or certain people's support, it makes no sense at all to stress over or give energy to it because, by doing so, you only give it power. Where Trump is concerned, he has known from the beginning that, although he would be running for president as a Republican, a great deal of Republicans would strongly oppose him. Therefore, instead of kissing their asses and begging for their support, even though he knows he could definitely use it, he publicly disdained them. Their attempts to thwart his presidential rise mean nothing because he is already powerful—and will surely gain more power without compromising his integrity for their endorsements and votes. If he were to compromise such and publicly announce his need for them, they would only mobilize against him in an even stronger capacity after having realized that Trump's dependence on them is a thumbscrew that they can use to their advantage. This is why Greene also points out that, when showing contempt for something that you cannot have, "the less interest you reveal, the more superior you seem," and this is what has put Trump in a much more superior position than virtually all of his opponents. And when you see him on television talking about how the "Establishment," the media, special interest groups and lobbyists are "against" him, and how the "system" is "rigged," most of the time, what you are seeing is this 36th Law in action.

Create Compelling Spectacles

Reporters often refer to the outstanding media coverage surrounding Donald Trump as a "media circus," and this is the direct result of the billionaire strategist continually creating compelling spectacles that keep everybody talking and wondering what is next. When Trump is in town, his entrance is always BIG and, when he speaks, he is bound to say something that sparks yet another round of controversy—and the mass media, addicted to high ratings, *always* seem to fall for it. The massive, and sometimes violent, anti-Trump protests at his rallies keeps the world hungering for more. The disgruntled man who jumped a barrier and rushed toward Trump onstage made headlines around the world, and Trump's Hitler-like salute at one of his rallies evoked fascist symbolism that pissed off Jews the world over (see "Abe Foxman: Trump Knew His Hitler-Like Salute Was Evoking Fascist Symbolism," at www. TheJewishWeek.com). This is typical Law 37 application, but those who have never studied *The 48 Laws of Power* do not even notice it, too driven by emotion to be convinced otherwise. Trump is a *master* at compelling-spectacle creation and, as long as the masses are hypnotically spellbound, mesmerized, emotionally affected by and negatively reacting to the startling imagery and shrewdly symbolic gestures used by Trump and his campaign, they will *never* understand his strategy.

Think as You Like but Behave Like Others

As much as many people do not want to accept it, the truth is that most people in any society are conventional to the point of being ridiculously predictable. If they are religious, they are confined to the precepts of their religion. If they are non-religious, they tend to have a disdain for religion in general. If they are "freethinkers," many of their interests are secular in nature, and much of their learning comes from self-help and ancient history-based books. And, if they are "political," their approach to politics is almost always conventional. Moreover, as intelligent as Trump is, it would be preposterous to say, or even think, that he does not know this. If he were unaware of it, he would not consistently have the upper hand on his opponents, and would simply think as they do. But such is not the case. Although, on the surface, it may seem as if he has a penchant for going against the times and outright bucking conventionality in an unorthodox fashion, the truth is that, in many ways, he is behaving like the masses. The masses, no matter what side of the political spectrum they are currently on, are dissatisfied with the direction in which America seems to be going, and Trump shrewdly embodies this dissatisfaction. Others believe that the political system is rigged, and Trump candidly agrees. Only a few people really know how he thinks and understand his strategies, and most of his supporters *believe* that they know and understand the same, which is why they are backing him with so much fervor. In their eyes, he is behaving just like them—or how they believe they *would* behave, if they could get away with it—and this alone is proof enough that Law 38 is being applied in full by The Donald.

Stir Up Waters to Catch Fish

When it comes to "stirring up waters to catch fish," or making enemies angry while staying calm in order to gain an advantage, Trump is among the most highly skilled at utilizing this strategy. For example, when he flew to California to campaign as the presumptive Republican nominee, after clinching the nomination with more delegates than needed, he remained calm during his rally while countless protesters were outside wreaking havoc in opposition to him, many of whom were spitting out expletives, while others were burning American flags. During the primaries, he also oftentimes remained calm while his political opponents were reacting to the waters he stirred against them, as if nothing that they said or did could even affect him, which heightened his appearance of superiority over them. He knows how to make people tick, and this has been well-documented by the mass media, which makes his application of this Law a public fact.

Despise the Free Lunch

The "free lunch" tactic is an age-old strategy that is still used by many in order to control others through obligation. People do this all the time, especially those who are wealthy and seek political power via campaign contributions. Rich people "buy" politicians all the time and, as aforementioned, Trump has even alluded to doing so himself. I remember him talking about this at a rally in Clear Lake, Iowa, when he said:

> *You know, it's interesting. I was looking at the ones I'm running against. I've contributed to most of them—can you believe it? I've contributed to most of them. And one of them said, "No, I don't think you've contributed to me." They found out I did. I contribute to everybody. I've given to Democrats. I've given to Hillary. I've given to everybody, because that was my job. I've got to give to them. because when I want something I get it. When I call, they kiss my ass. It's true. They kiss my ass. It's true.*

But, when it comes to people "buying" *Trump* through campaign contributions, he is not having it. Why? Because *no one* can buy a true boss, and by doing his own thing with his own money, he himself remains the shot caller. He takes contributions, but only those that come with no strings attached, from people who want nothing in return, and this is public knowledge. The fact that he disdains the free lunch, especially from lobbyists, is proof that he keeps this Law in execution—and only a mastermind would do such.

Laws 41-48
Avoid Stepping into a Great Man's Shoes

One of the greatest men that Trump has ever known was his own father, Fred Trump, who made his own great fortune by thinking BIG. In spite of the controversies regarding his alleged arrest at a KKK rally in 1927, and his refusal to rent his apartments to black people back in the day, the fact remains that he was a real estate genius who made history in business, and gave birth to a prodigal son who surpassed him by leaps and bounds. History has proven that the children of great men and women tend to walk in the shoes of their parents, never setting themselves apart by doing something different that results in greatness, so they never really gain the respect of The People. Instead of forging their own identities, they live in their parents' shadows. We see examples of this all the time. When Lisa Marie Presley, Elvis' daughter, released a pop album, her music was okay, but not enough to eclipse the works of her father. The same is true of Sean Lennon, son of John Lennon from the Beatles. And Albert Einstein's son, Hans Albert, was a pretty brilliant professor and scientist, but was never able to come up with a major theory of his own that would surpass his father's theory of relativity. All of these people have tried to step into a great man's shoes, but failed. However, Trump has never violated this Law. He has taken his legacy to the next level. Everything that his father did with real estate, Trump has done bigger and better. His father's empire was worth hundreds of millions; Trump's, a few billion. And Trump's major success at branding, Reality TV and politics completely set him apart from his father, although his dad does deserve credit for showing him the ropes; teaching him what management, leadership and persistence truly is; and letting him do his own thing. Now, after reinventing himself, Trump is in a different bracket of individuals who have evaded parental shadowing by creating their own greatness, their own way. Jay-Z, Beyoncé, Kanye West, Kim Kardashian, Miley Cyrus, Angelina Jolie and even George W. Bush are all members of this bracket. Say what you will about them but, at the end of the day, they absolutely *refuse* to live in anyone's shadow. This is yet another Law that Trump naturally applies.

Strike the Shepherd and the Sheep Will Scatter

When I think about Trump applying this Law, what comes to mind is what he once said in response to a question posed to him by Oprah on her talk show. Oprah asked him, "Do you remember the first time you had to fire somebody, Donald?" He did, in fact, talk about how he remembered that, but what caught a lot of peoples' attention was what he said about the kind of people he *loves* to fire—and then "go after afterwards." You can watch a video clip of this on Oprah.com, but here is some of what he said in response to Oprah's question:

> I do, I do. I was doing deals. I was going to the Wharton School of Finance...and somebody was not doing a good job, and I had to terminate that person. And I did it. I mean, it's business. You do it. You have to do it...I don't love doing it. You know, the concept of firing is not a very pleasant thing, and I don't like doing it. You know, as I've said before, I love doing it if somebody really, really deserves it. If they've been bad, if they've been disloyal, if they've been thieves, if they've been doing something, I don't mind it at all—that's fine. And not only that, go after them afterwards. I, you know...take it to the full extent.

This resonated with me because I could definitely relate to one having to deal with snakes in the workplace. One foul-mouthed, devious serpent in the workplace can contaminate the minds of a dozen employees in no time, so it is always best to get rid of them and kill their influence. The same thing occurs in life with so-called friends, as well as in politics, and no person in a powerful position such as Trump's, man or woman, can sustain an empire without having to occasionally, and sometimes constantly, rid their domains of snakes. Even Oprah herself is not exempt, in spite of her exaggerated public image. If you are too Oprah-conditioned to understand this, then author Kitty Kelley's groundbreaking book *Oprah: A Biography* would do you some justice. But, as for Trump, if he has had to scatter sheep in the workplace by striking shepherds with wicked intentions, just imagine what he has to do in the world of politics and power in general. We have already seen him scatter the countless sheep of his political opponents during the primaries, and this alone is enough proof of Trump's utilization of this 42nd Law.

Work On the Hearts and Minds of Others

Most people are either too stubborn to admit it but, as I have said before, Donald Trump is a master seducer, and this is why his hold on the world is so great. The mass media has society brainwashed, believing that seduction primarily deals with love and romance, when the truth is that it is just a psychological game of persuasion. When one knows how people think, it makes it easy to persuade them. And Donald Trump has this skill down to a science. In fact, I remember seeing a book once on Amazon.com that Trump allegedly co-authored with Bill Gates entitled *The 48 Laws of Power and Their Impact on My Life*. However, the page itself said that the book was out of print due to limited availability, and the only customer review that I remember seeing claimed that it was a fake book. I have not looked any further into it, though, because I am already convinced by Trump's actions alone that he is a master executer of the 48 Laws. But, if he and Gates actually co-authored such a book, although I do not need it for claim verification, it would definitely prove my assertions to others who take Trump for a dummy. As far as this particular Law is concerned, even former GOP spokeswoman Virginia Hume understands Trump's mastery at seduction, though, by her own admission, she initially believed he was an idiot. Now, she says, "I've recently learned, however, that Donald Trump is not an idiot. He might even be a genius." Her article, "Donald Trump, Master Seducer: The Vitamin Scam, the Art of Seduction and Rick Santorum: How I Finally Understood the Trump Phenomenon," which I read about on Medium. com, is something I think all Democrats, Republicans, Independents and anti-Trump protesters should read, if they desire, in any way, to understand The Donald. The point is that he has gotten where he is now by working on the hearts and minds of others, and I seriously doubt that this will stop anytime soon, because ceasing to apply this Law this far ahead in the game would not be a good strategy at all.

Disarm and Infuriate with The Mirror Effect

In reference to this Law, as it applies to one's enemies, Robert Greene says the following: "By holding up a mirror to their psyches, you seduce them with the illusion that you share their values; by holding up a mirror to their actions, you teach them a lesson." All of us are guilty of doing this at some point in our lives in order to get whatever it was that we wanted— or to teach someone who messed with us a lesson. As for Trump, it seems as if this is one of the Laws he applies all the time. He has a knack for using the mirror effect when people attack him, and when he strikes back, almost *all* of his enemies fall. A CNN article by Gregory Krieg entitled "When Trump Hits Back, He Hits Back Hard" actually talks about this, in so many words. An excerpt from this article says:

> *In Donald Trump's world, an "eye for an eye" doesn't quite cut it. His calculus is much more severe—even a modest political jab or unflattering piece of reporting is likely to be met with unrelenting force. Trump met criticism from his Republican opponents with mocking nicknames and scornful insults. But it didn't stop there. Using the same tactics with reporters, he has often responded to tough or probing questions—as he did during a fraught exchange on Tuesday—with angry, often personal, attacks.*

And most of Trump's adversaries end up overreacting when he does to them what they tried to do to him, but he ended up doing better. Another example of Trump applying this Law is how he dealt with former governor Mitt Romney, who attacked him and called him a "phony" (see "Trump Responds, In Kind, to Romney as a 'Disaster' and 'Choke Artist,'" by Menachem Rephun, on www.jpupdates.com). Where this particular Law is concerned, Trump is the John "Bones" Jones of strategy. Either it is just me, or it seems as if Romney is now keeping a low profile because he is afraid of Trump's wrath. He has already been knocked out once, and another blow from The Donald may just send him over a suicidal edge. Instead of putting up one mirror, Trump puts up a thousand, and it is extremely rare to find any opponent who can handle such powerful reflection.

Preach the Need for Change, but Never Reform Too Much at Once

Proof of Trump's application of this 45th Law is found on the fact that he absolutely refuses to conform to orthodox political and even religious ideology, and unabashedly goes against the status quo, approaching politics in a way that has never really been done before—all the while preaching the need for practical change in a way that meshes with principles from the "old school." And this is exactly why young, middle-aged and older voters all support him. Psychology teaches us that young people typically disdain *anything* traditional, because their generation wants to do its own thing; middle-aged people are more mature and impartial in important matters, because they are stuck in the middle of the age bracket and can relate to both sides, the young and the old; and old people are typically stuck in their ways because, as they approach demise, they begin to view life in terms of how many years they have left, and they are sustained by memories of the times that they grew up in. Most importantly, though, as the old saying goes, as people get older, they eventually realize that "there is nothing new under the sun," and the younger generation's "advancements" are only minor improvements on the past. So, old folks do not have time to waste on stuff that they already know. Therefore, in the game of power, any power player who wants to excel at power has to appeal to the young, the middle-aged and the old, and this is something that Trump has mastered doing. His radical personality and lavish lifestyle appeal to the youth; his maturity and mid-life development appeal to the middle-aged; and his "Make America Great Again" slogan appeals to many of those in the older demographic who want America to "be the way it used to be." As long as Trump's campaign continues to operate within these parameters, Law 45 will take care of itself.

Never Appear Too Perfect

At this point, it is pretty much a known fact that Donald Trump is far from perfect. In fact, after having been meet with considerable opposition from haters for most of his life, and becoming cognizant of his own strengths and imperfections, I seriously doubt that he would ever waste his time trying to be so. Virtually every person in life, in general, especially in this country, attracts a million enemies for simply trying to be perfect, or appear as such. When haters cannot really find any dirt on you, they will dig deeper and deeper until they can find some. And, if they come up empty-handed, jealousy and envy will cause them to start fabricating stories and using dirty tactics in an effort to sabotage the success of the person they hate so much. To survive all of that as a billionaire, maintain his power base and excel in politics, Trump obviously knows how to avoid the pitfall of appearing too perfect, which explains why he absolutely refuses to appear so. Look at what he said in *The Art of the Deal* way back in 1987:

> *One of the problems when you become successful is that jealousy and envy inevitably follow. There are people—I categorize them as life's losers—who get their sense of accomplishment and achievement from trying to stop others. As far as I'm concerned, if they had any real ability, they wouldn't be fighting me, they'd be doing something constructive themselves.*

In this world, most people, unless brainwashed by religion, know that they can never be perfect, no matter how much they try to be. They have heard about Jesus, but know that they could never be just like him. So, when successful people come along who seem to have no flaws, as if they were the Messiah, these people are marked for crucifixion. Trump is already a target just from him being him and outshining almost everyone around him, so it would be foolish for him to suddenly start trying to appear perfect. Every now and then, when he "fucks up," he takes the humane approach and apologizes, and this makes a lot of people respect him, haters included—all because he has flaws that he is not afraid to own up to. Those flaws and apologies are proof that Trump abides by this Law. He is not God—he is a man, like the rest of us.

Do Not Go Past the Mark You Aimed for;
In Victory, Learn When to Stop

In spite of the common misconception that Trump is a hotheaded egomaniac who lets victory go to his head, the truth is that Trump is so shrewd at applying this Law that he can switch from boisterous to calm faster than Reverend Al Sharpton can go from walking to marching, all while staying focused on what the bigger goal is. An example of this is how he conducted himself at his Republican primary night event at the Trump National Golf Club in Briarcliff Manor, New York, after victoriously making it to the top of his political party. Many people thought that he would come out brash and offensive when it was time for him to speak. They thought he would brag about his victory. However, he did not do any of this. Instead, he came out "presidential" and focused on the unification of his party, which awed many people who thought they had him figured out. Here is some of what Ashley Parker and Maggie Haberman of the *New York Times* had to say about it in their article "Donald Trump Softens His Tone, and the G.O.P. Hopes It Will Last," published in June:

> *BRIARCLIFF MANOR, N.Y. — Donald J. Trump, aided by two teleprompters, presented the version of himself on Tuesday evening that Republican Party officials had desperately craved—softer, serious and sophisticated.*
>
> *"I understand the responsibility of carrying the mantle and I will never ever let you down," Mr. Trump said in a speech at his golf club here. "I will make you proud of your party and our movement."*
>
> *Mr. Trump's disciplined performance was geared at soothing nervous voters and at stopping the flight of high-ranking Republicans. And it came just hours after Mr. Trump reminded them why they had been concerned in the first place.*

No doubt about it, Trump definitely loves to kick ass and make his victories known, but he never lets victory throw him off his game. After kicking ass, when a mission is accomplished, instead of going too far, he stops and "keeps it moving," headed toward something else, while most of his opponents defeat themselves by violating this Law. This is not the result of coincidence—it is the result of well-planned strategy.

Assume Formlessness

Being formless is having no obvious plan that can make you easily susceptible to enemy attacks. As I have mentioned throughout this chapter, Trump is an enigma in politics. No one seems able to figure out his strategy, and no one truly understands him. Most politicians are like other politicians, but Trump is only like himself, and he is always on the move, changing form, like a chameleon. By assuming formlessness, he keeps his enemies confused and at bay. They spend so much time reacting to him and trying to figure him out that they end up perpetually behind and unable to affect him, unconsciously yielding him the advantage. That which has no form is virtually impossible to defeat, and this is why we are still witnessing The Donald fly high at the top of the political arena.

After so many years among snakes, political or otherwise, Trump has reached a level of strategic insight that only a few will ever experience or understand. Whether we like it or not, his *actions* show us that he is a master of the power game. If such were not the case, he would have tasted defeat a long time ago. Only masterful power players can make it this far and still remain on top of their game. The Laws mentioned here, all 48 of them, have become so second nature to Trump that he oftentimes executes strategy by instinct, while others rely on a team of advisors to *tell* them what to do. Where this man is concerned, it is time for society and the world to wake up and realize what kind of mastermind they are dealing with. Nothing positive will ever come from unifying against him, even if he *loses* the election, because power is power, and some people are not meant to be played with. Only conditioned minds that are out of tune with reality would call for an alternative to Donald Trump, when there *is* none. And, if you are under the impression that Hillary Clinton is the alternative, and she were to be elected, after the initial fanfare following her historic achievement and little progress is made by her hand, as reality begins to rear its ugly head and her power begins to slip from her grasp, you will see exactly why Donald Trump should have been your initial choice. And it will have absolutely nothing to do with Clinton being a woman.

The point is that many of us have seriously underestimated Donald Trump, he has mastered the power game, is definitely a force to be reckoned with—and he will not be going anywhere anytime soon. If you hate him, you need to free yourself from negative emotion and learn to "let go." If you do not agree with him, he does not care, and you should learn to "agree to disagree." And, if you truly care about your country, then, you need to wake up and realize what kind of world you are living in, then aim to elect a president who is cognizant of the same, embraces it, and is ready to make the tough decisions that most politicians circumvent for financial gain, and to maintain the illusion of peace and order on a very fucked up earth—an earth where massacres like the recent one in Orlando, Florida, are the direct result of greed, cowardice, weak-willed decision making and bad leadership in politics. But a truly powerful mastermind who understands the above Laws can take America and the world to the next level. That man's name is Donald J. Trump. If we allow social and political conditioning to convince us not to vote for him, the Great American Illusion will continue until its downfall by its own hand. By making America *great* again, we will make America *safe* again. If ever this truth is collectively realized, The People will make the right decision. Until then, it is time to wake up. The question is: What in the hell are *you* going to do?

2

The Machiavellian Mindset: Princes and Peasants

Most of the people around you are Peasants residing in a world that is run by Princes, and this is a reality you need to face if you want to understand power and politics. When I speak of princes, I am not talking about the sons of monarchs or male royal rulers of small states. I am talking about people with power in general, male and female. When I mention peasants, I am simply referring to people with low social status—a class that the world's majority falls into. Princes are those at the top (royal families, multimillionaires and billionaires, presidents and other world leaders, and those who have acquired great influence via fame and notoriety), and Peasants are those on the bottom, that is, the masses. Even those who happen to fall in the middle are Peasants, too, because they have not quite made it to the top yet. The biggest misconception about achieving Prince status is that, once you make it, everything else that you want will automatically fall into place, as if your empire would run itself. This is why, time and time again, many of the people who quickly reach the top fall back down just as quickly as they went up. And, almost always, when you pay attention to their fall from grace, eventually, you realize that their fall had absolutely nothing to do with fate or the gods—they just did not know how to play the game. If they did know, they were just too weak and timid to play it.

When you become rich or famous, influence inevitably follows, because the world is full of discontent people who, on some level, desire wealth and attention. And these people will flock to you, only seeing what could be gained for themselves through their association with you. Most people who make it take advantage of this in some way, because such is necessary in order to keep a fan base and, especially, to build and run an empire. But, at a certain point, this influence becomes *power* and, when power comes, so do enemies—and this is the level of the game where most powerful people fail. At this point, the game gets dirty, and the use of basic strategy is not enough to survive. People you do not even know will come straight at you with intentions to tear your empire down to the ground, while others work silently against you in secret, patiently awaiting your downfall. Many of your friends will become your enemies as well, and all of this opposition will be driven by vicious, malicious seeds of jealousy and envy that you may never understand. It just comes with the territory, and the only way to survive it is to ditch emotion, accept the fact that you are at war, and play the game. This is what any true Prince would do, because only a Prince with a Peasant mindset would do everything in his power to avoid such.

Where Donald Trump is concerned, it is a well-known fact that he is far from a Peasant and undoubtedly a Prince, and one who, as I have shown in the previous chapter, knows how to play the political power game. As I have mentioned, while most people simply perceive him as an arrogant celebrity billionaire with a huge ego and bigotry problem, there is more to this man than meets the eye. From my study and observation, and simply due to my profound understanding of power itself, I have found that Donald Trump is a vastly intelligent, master strategist who approaches life, business and politics with a warrior mindset that is extremely underestimated by the masses. He not only thinks like a Prince but is also a known "student" of Machiavelli, that is, Niccolò Machiavelli, the famous political strategist and author of *The Prince*, the political treatise that is the backbone of American politics. Doubt him if you want to, but Donald Trump is a motherfucking genius. And time will reveal everything that I am telling you in this book.

One of the biggest mistakes that many critics make in regard to Donald and *The Prince* is the drawing of comparisons between Trump and Machiavelli. They say that, if Machiavelli were still alive today, he would disagree with many of Trump's strategies, because he does not always abide by the tenets put forth by Machiavelli. But I strongly disagree. When *The Prince* was written and published back in the 1500s, during the Renaissance period in Italy, the political game was being played more strictly than it is today, due to the moral and political environment of that particular time. But the times have changed, morality has *long* flown out of the political window, the game has evolved, and Trump understands this. As an *age-of-the-sage.org* article entitled "Niccolò Machiavelli—The Prince" points out, Machiavelli believed that "a ruler is not constrained by traditional ethical norms. In his view, a prince should be concerned only with power and be bound only by rules that would lead to success in political actions." When we look at Trump and see him bucking traditional ethical norms, the notion that this somehow makes him un-Machiavellian is proven a lie, because Machiavelli himself would *want* Trump to defy normality. Additionally, he would be *proud* of Trump for executing all of the unorthodox strategies that he had already known would bring him to power. Therefore, if Machiavelli were still alive to this day, rather than oppose Trump, after seeing how masterfully he plays the game, he would probably be his *advisor*.

Now, I have taken an in-depth look at a lot of these critics' comments, and I am convinced that a lot of their articles and comments are mostly driven by both a desire to ride the Trump wave in an effort to make a dollar—and pure nonsense. However, to prove my point even further, I knocked the dust off an old book that I fell in love with more than a decade ago, when I decided to take my then general understanding of power and politics to a much greater level. And this book was a copy of *The Prince*, which I have reread, in its entirety, a total of six times, with the intention of discovering what the hell these critics are talking about. And, every single time that I read it, I realized more and more just how stupid most of these critics are. They remind me of those uber-traditional, super Old School Christians who take Biblical texts from a different time *way* too seriously and, then, get mad at the New Age Christians for changing with the times. Most of those old Biblical laws do not even apply anymore, and the same is true concerning some of the tenets laid down by Machiavelli in *The Prince*. Trump only applies what is useful *today*, and all of that other stuff is for the birds. Nevertheless, I want you to see this for yourself, so, here are a few excerpts from the book that describe Trump to a T, making it known that he is definitely a Prince who is meant for power, because he has truly mastered the game.

In Chapter XIV of *The Prince*, entitled "That Which Concerns a Prince On the Subject of the Art of War," Machiavelli discusses how a Prince should dedicate himself to the study of war, its rules and its discipline. Here is what he says:

> *A prince ought to have no other aim or thought, nor select anything else for his study, than war and its rules and discipline; for this is the sole art that belongs to him who rules, and it is of such force that it not only upholds those who are born princes, but it often enables men to rise from a private station to that rank. And, on the contrary, it is seen that when princes have thought more of ease than of arms they have lost their states. And the first cause of you losing it is to neglect this art; and what enables you to acquire a state is to be master of the art.*

It seems as if every time we see Trump in the media, he is engaged in some kind of battle. He is either being attacked from all angles imaginable or counterattacking his enemies and, because of this, he has to keep his mind in warrior mode at all times. But he has been in this state of mind long before he even officially hit the scene running for president, and signs of this are made evident, for example, in virtually every book that he has ever written or co-written. This lets us know that he had already been in this state of mind when he decided to enter the race for the White House. He entered it from a private station, as an independent businessman with no real "political" power, and strategically slaughtered his opponents, whose approaches to politics were relegated to political tradition—while, on the contrary, his approach was more like all-out war. His enemies disdained his approach, totally underestimated his unconventional strategy and neglected the art of war. By doing so, they handed over to him the delegates needed to clench the Republican presidential nomination and "lost their states." And this is when Trump officially rose to power. As you can see, if you have been following the 2016 election, Trump's approach to politics was, and still is, in alignment with what Machiavelli says about the success that comes from a Prince's dedication to, and study of, the art of war. So, how can critics who consider themselves intelligent even dispute and deny this?

In this chapter, Machiavelli also says the following in regard to a Prince:

As regards action, he ought above all things to keep his men well organized and drilled, to follow incessantly the chase, by which he accustoms his body to hardships, and learns something of the nature of localities, and gets to find out how the valleys open out, how the plains lie, and to understand the nature of rivers and marshes, and in all this to take the greatest care. Which knowledge is useful in two ways. Firstly, he learns to know his country, and is better able to undertake its defence; afterwards, by means of the knowledge and observation of that locality, he understands with ease any other which it may be necessary for him to study hereafter; because the hills, valleys, and plains, and rivers and marshes that are, for instance, in Tuscany, have a certain resemblance to those of other countries, so that with a knowledge of the aspect of one country one can easily arrive at a knowledge of others. And the prince that lacks this skill lacks the essential which it is desirable that a captain should possess, for it teaches him to surprise his enemy, to select quarters, to lead armies, to array the battle, to besiege towns to advantage.

Now, for one moment, I want you to think about Trump's campaign, his tough demeanor and his world travels when on business and vacation. His campaign workers go extremely hard for him and are very well-organized and drilled, in spite of a little former confusion that led to the firing of Corey Lewandowski, his previous campaign manager. And their work has been known to pay off big time, resulting in cross-cultural voter turnouts that have shocked the nation time and time again. As for his demeanor, though he can be friendly at times, he is cold and calculating to such a point that nothing can really affect him and throw him off his game, which makes him a formidable opponent. And, as for his world travels, Trump has been to virtually every major country in the world and, while there, had the opportunity to not only build big business relationships with reputable leaders and entrepreneurs, but also gauge the states of foreign territories and the psychology of the people inhabiting the many lands that he has visited. In this way, over the years, he has been able to gain a lot of the same experience that a typical Secretary of State has, and this has taken his understanding of foreign localities to another level above that of the common citizenry. Common politicians believe that a president must have past experience in foreign relations under a government entity in order to deal with affairs, but this reasoning is flat out ridiculous because, if one already has a track record of calling shots overseas, independent of government or not, he or she is already qualified to deal with foreign relations, and Donald Trump already meets these standards, as Machiavelli says a Prince should.

In Chapter XV, entitled "Concerning Things for Which Men and Especially Princes Are Praised or Blamed," it seems as if Machiavelli is referring to Trump directly, which makes Trump's aforementioned alignment with Machiavelli's teachings even more obvious. Here is what he says:

> *Therefore, putting on one side imaginary things concerning a prince and discussing those which are real, I say that all men when they are spoken of, and chiefly princes for being more highly placed, are remarkable for some of those qualities which bring them either blame or praise. Thus one has the reputation of being liberal, another mean. One is said to be generous, one greedy; one cruel, one kind; one disloyal, another faithful; one weak and cowardly, another bold and brave; one friendly, another proud; one pleasure loving, another restrained; one sincere, another not truthful; one hard, another easy; one serious, another foolish; one religious, another unbelieving, and the like. And I know that everyone will confess that it would be most worthy in a prince to exhibit all the above qualities that are considered good. But, because they can neither be entirely possessed nor observed in any one person, for human conditions do not permit it, it is necessary for him to be sufficiently careful so that he may know how to avoid the criticism of those things considered bad which would lose him his state. Also, he should avoid, if it is possible, bad behavior which would not lose him his state, but, if this is not possible, he may with less hesitation do it. Moreover, he need not feel uneasy about*

being criticized for that bad behavior which is necessary to maintain the state, because if everything is considered carefully, it will be found that something which looks like virtue, if followed would be his ruin; while something else, which looks wrong, may bring him security and wealth.

We all know that Trump is a highly praised and controversial figure. On one hand, he is often praised for his major accomplishments in business, as well his accomplishments as a writer. On the other, oftentimes, he is blamed for the backlash and chaos that typically result from him simply speaking his mind, especially about sensitive issues that many people take very seriously, but that he himself seems to not give a damn about when he is in counterattack mode. But, here is the thing. In spite of his qualities that can be considered good or bad, when it comes to political strategy, instead of going so far in the negative in a way that would "lose him his state," he keeps these qualities balanced. Good or bad, he uses whichever quality is best when necessity requires him to do so and, by strategizing in this manner, he is able to maintain his security and wealth, just as Machiavelli says shall happen to such a Prince.

Now, pay attention to some of Machiavelli's wisdom from Chapter XVII, "Concerning Cruelty and Clemency, and Whether It Is Better to Be Loved Than Feared." Machiavelli declares:

And of all princes, it is impossible for the new prince to avoid the reputation for cruelty. This is because new states are full of dangers. Nevertheless a prince ought to be slow to believe and to act, and should not show fear. He should proceed in a calm manner with care and concern for others, so that too much confidence does not make him careless and too much distrust does not make him always suspicious. Related to this a question arises: whether it be better to be loved than feared or feared than loved? It may be answered that one should wish to be both, but, because it is difficult to unite them in one person it is much safer to be feared than loved, when only one is possible. The reason for this is that in general men are ungrateful, inconstant, false, cowardly, and greedy. As long as you succeed, they are yours entirely; they will offer you their blood, property, life, and children, when the need is far distant. But when the need approaches, they turn against you. A prince who, relying entirely on their promises, has neglected other ways of protecting himself, will be ruined. Friendships that are obtained by payments, and not by greatness or nobility of mind, may indeed be earned, but they are not secured, and in time of need cannot be relied upon. Men are less worried about offending one who is loved than one who is feared. Love is preserved by the link of gratefulness which, owing to the weak nature of men, is broken at every opportunity for their advantage; but fear preserves you by a fear of punishment which never fails... Returning to the question of being feared or loved, I come to the conclusion that, because men love according to their own will and fear according to the will of the prince, a wise prince should establish himself on that which is in his own control and not in the control of others. He must try however to avoid hatred.

As a new Prince on the political scene, much has been said by critics in regard to Trump's so-called reputation for cruelty. Said cruelty is largely based on Trump's comments about Mexicans and Muslims, the crack he made about Megyn Kelly, his alleged sanctioning of violence at his rallies, and his assumed degradation of women. Because the new state of American politics is full of dangers, as is America due to foreign and domestic violence that threaten our national security, it is easy for critics to paint Trump as a cruel politician who, if elected in November, would become a cruel president. But, no matter how hard anti-Trump critics try to brainwash the American people into believing this propaganda, their attempts always fail, because Trump is smart enough to apologize from time to time when his behavior offends too many people. And he does so in a manner that causes many people to forgive him. Of course, some people definitely hate him, but most people who oppose him do not seriously abhor him because, if they did, he would most certainly already be a dead man. They do not hate him—they just fear and dislike him, for various reasons. But Trump could not care less, because he himself already knows that it is better to be feared than loved, and his perspective is that "it is better to be respected than both," as he once told Eric Bolling on The O'Reilly Factor (see "Trump Talks Foreign Policy: 'I'd Rather Be

Respected' Than Loved" on Fox News Insider). And these facts are proof of Trump's "Machiavellianistic" propensities.

And, lastly, in Chapter XXI, "How A Prince Should Conduct Himself as to Gain Renown," Machiavelli says something that is so simple, yet so profound, that it makes one's understanding of Trump's rise a no-brainer. Machiavelli states:

> *Nothing makes a prince so esteemed as great enterprises and setting a fine example.*

Trump is the king of great enterprise and setting fine examples. The Trump Organization, a privately owned, international conglomerate, is one of the most successful and respected organizations in the world, and even the stoniest critics cannot refute this. A fine example has already been set by Trump's success in business alone, which makes him a Prince in his own right. As far as esteem goes, the man has earned a star on the Hollywood Walk of Fame, an achievement that is a testament to his power and influence. So, to all of you critics who attest that Donald Trump is anything but Machiavellian, I say *¡Chúpame la verga!* It seems as if you are too stupid to do anything else.

The Key Differences between Masterminds and Conventionalists

Let us begin with conventionalists. Aside from Donald Trump's critics particularly, the larger issue at hand regarding politics and The People is conventionalism and the dumbing down of society. The wisest people of old, on every continent, thought for themselves, were able to devote sufficient time to self-actualization studies conducted in solitude, without much distraction, and sagacity was the result of this. However, nowadays, self-actualization is virtually non-existent among the world's citizenry, especially here in America, due to all of the ridiculous distractions that, collectively, make up what I like to call the "Social Matrix." People do not really read anymore, and if they do, it is either the tabloids, something concerning entertainment, eye-catching headlines in the newspaper or, simply, a novel, none of which have any profound degree of realism. And most of the political publications that people read, regardless of party affiliation, are predicated on a modern model of political thought that has gotten away from its origin. Conventionalists go with the trends and ideology sparked by masterminds who dictate the course of society via shrewd strategy incorporated into everything that the public has been taught and conditioned to regard dearly. Although they believe that they are thinking for themselves and are in full control of their minds, the truth is that their thinking processes have been manipulated by societal mind crafters whose only interest is social brainwashing that results in profitable ignorance, and this truth only escapes those who are still caught up in the Social Matrix. At any rate, in addition to undertaking study of strategy and seduction, as discussed in the preceding chapter, those who seek to understand Donald Trump must also become aware of the basic psychological differences between masterminds and conventionalists. And here is what psychology teaches us about the two.

If you have never heard of the late psychologist Lawrence Kohlberg, one of the 20th Century's most eminent psychologists, you should google him and study some of his work, especially his theory on the stages of moral development, which is a noteworthy adaptation of a psychological theory originally conceived by the late, renowned Swiss psychologist Jean Piaget. According to Wikipedia, Kohlberg's theory "holds that moral reasoning, the basis for ethical behavior, has six identifiable developmental stages, each more adequate at responding to moral dilemmas than its predecessor." Kohlberg "followed the development of moral judgment far beyond the ages studied earlier by Piaget, who also claimed that logic and morality develop through constructive stages." And these six stages of moral development "are grouped into three levels: pre-conventional morality [stages one and two], conventional morality [stages three and four], and post-conventional morality [stages five and six]."

In stage one, which is obedience- and punishment-driven, people refuse to do something because they believe it is wrong and the consequences could result in punishment. I know a lot of people who seem to have been stuck in this stage forever, people with big dreams, huge talent and big ideas, but who absolutely refuse to take action due to fear of criticism, controversy and failure. They believe that it would be wrong for them to publicly reveal how they truly feel and, if they were to do so, they would be punished by society via negative backlash. Some of these people are entertainers and writers whose talent and skill would surely make them successful if they ever decide to pursue their dreams, but their fear of "punishment" keeps them unsuccessful, and they want to obey the status quo to such an extent that they will *never* be successful. Thus, they remain ignorant and will never reach the mastermind level.

In stage two, which is self-interest driven, people only care about themselves and seem to be on a perpetual search for incentives. These are the types that will sell you out for a dollar, even if it means getting you in deep trouble with your worst enemies, or even the authorities, so that they can take over your position or gain favor from those who hate you the most. I know a million people like this, and quite a number of them run in circles that prey on people with status of some kind. They are petty and greedy and care about no one but themselves.

Stage three, which deals with people's "good" intentions as determined by social consensus, is about individuals who "enter society by conforming to social standards" and are "receptive to approval or disapproval from others as it reflects society's views." In particular, this stage references those among us who strive to become "good boys" and "good girls" after discovering that societal goodness brings certain societal benefits. They do not want to be naughty—they want to be nice and thought well of. These are the types that suppress their deepest urges while on a quest to be socially "perfect," and who do everything in their power to run from reality, especially during debates. I have seen this time and time again, with my own eyes, especially in church. The ironic thing, though, to add weight to the matter, is that, for me, when it came to dating people in this stage, the most holier-than-thou "believers" turned out to be the wildest, most sexually satisfying women I have ever had in bed, which was due to them unconventionally "letting go" and allowing themselves to be free for a moment. However, after a while, they almost always reverted to their conventional ways, believing that letting go was somehow socially wrong, resulting in me realizing just how brainwashed they were, and eventually cutting them off. People rarely break free from this stage and, if you end up growing attached to them during their short-lived hiatus from traditionalism, the hardest thing in the world is letting them go.

Stage four is driven by authority and social order obedience. This is a state in which obeying "laws, dictums and social conventions" is important because of "their importance in maintaining a functioning society." In this stage, people no longer need individual approval, because "moral" reasoning, by societal definition, guides their thinking, but only on a skewed level that causes them to associate the so-called wrongdoing of one with the mindset of all. They want to uphold societal laws and rules, but only in a subjective manner that does not take justice and human rights into the equation. To these types, the laws and rules are fixed and should be obeyed at all cost, even if these social imperatives have been biased and unfair since their conception. The code of morality these people live by "is still predominantly dictated by an outside force," and they are simply too blind to see it.

Now, stages five and six mark the beginning of unconventional mental development. Stage four is "social contract driven," a state in which laws are regarded as social contracts; the opinions, rights and values of others are taken into serious consideration; and "the greatest good for the greatest number of people" becomes one's focus. By my own observation, people who spend an exorbitant amount of time participating in nonviolent "justice" and "equality" rallies and protests are a decent example of this. In stage five, however, "moral reasoning is based on abstract reasoning using universal ethical principles." People in this stage feel seriously committed to justice and feel *obligated* to disobey unjust laws and rules. People in this stage take action in order to do what is right, without fear of punishment or anything else. Most people never make it to this stage, but some do. The majority, nonetheless, typically remain stuck in the first four stages, thus remaining slaves to convention. They *never* reach the mastermind level. My observation of people in this final stage has shown that, for example, where protest is concerned, whereas those in the fifth stage are more nonviolent, stage sixers have a tendency to become radical in protest, sometimes to the point of being violent. However, said violence often occurs during the heat of passion and is rarely intentional. These people are passionate about doing what is right and having unfair laws do the same and, when angered by those who go too far in their efforts to justify unfairness, in the heat of the moment, some of them snap, and rightly so. Moreover, where Donald Trump is concerned, he is definitely in stage *seven*—a world of his own. This is because, like all masterminds, he is just too unique, unconventional and advanced to fit into *any* of these categories, although, when he was much younger, he most likely exhibited traits that corresponded with the above stages. However, those days are long gone. When Trump entered the mastermind domain, his mental development took off like an extraterrestrial rocket, and he has been advancing ever since. With that said, let us now shift the discussion to the psychology of masterminds.

Mastermind Psychology

One of the biggest lies in America is that a person's brainpower can be measured by his or her IQ and academic accomplishments, as if standardized tests and holding a bunch of degrees or prestigious positions make one uber-intelligent. But I have never subscribed to this notion, because some of the dumbest people I know personally are college graduates with decent-to-high IQs—and the shrewdest people I know, believe it or not, have neither. Having a high IQ, or even a PhD, does not make one intelligent. By definition, intelligence is "the ability to acquire and apply knowledge and skills," but masterminds are those who do this on an *advanced* level predicated on *strategy*. Although Trump has spent some time in college, from my observation, aside from his father's sake, as a strategist who understood how people *associate* a degree with intelligence, he only entered the collegiate arena to test himself among the "best" and use his degree to his advantage. He knew he was intelligent long before he had even entered college. If Trump were a conventional person who believed that a degree would make him intelligent, surely, he would have devoted most of his time to his studies and on-campus activities. However, this was not the case, as a Brendan Morrow article on www.heavynews.com revealed back in May 2016.

In Morrow's article, "Where Did Donald Trump Go to College? 5 Fast Facts You Need to Know," he talks about how Trump did not really graduate with honors, how 12 of Trump's 13 classmates had no recollection of The Donald whatsoever, how Trump was not very involved on campus, and how "he showed up for classes and did what was required of him, but he was clearly bored and spent a lot of time on outside business activities." As you can see, although Trump attended college, college was not his passion—it was business that moved him. Thus, for a mastermind like Donald, college was nothing more than a means to an end. He even states in *The Art of the Deal* that a degree from the Wharton School of Finance "doesn't prove very much," and this helps us peer into the true nature of his mind.

As far as behavior and psychology go, masterminds tend to be more logical, assertive, fast- paced, efficient, results-oriented and very politically incorrect. Whatever they are doing, they cut through all of the bullshit and get straight to the point. This has nothing to do with arrogance and conceit. They already know what you know, just on another level that you do not yet understand, and already have their master plan figured out. Therefore, unless strategy is involved, masterminds do not have time to waste on shit that they already know, and they tend to know more about people than people know about themselves. In power, they often avoid appearing too smart, because downplayed intelligence results in underestimation that multiplies opportunities for maneuverability. They never reveal their true way of thinking, will never tell you what their true weaknesses are, and are proficient at using enemies without asking them for favors, whereas conventionalists tend to always want something in return. The traits and behavior of masterminds are totally atypical, unlike those of conventionalists.

Conventional people are like clones; masterminds are *different*, oftentimes to the point of seeming strange and, sometimes, flat out crazy. When pursuing something, conventionalists tend to overanalyze, procrastinate and follow the blueprint of others. Masterminds, contrarily, devise *strategic* plans and make it their mission to execute them at all cost. Additionally, masterminds are so advanced in their thinking that it is virtually impossible to find one who is devoutly religious; uninformed on subjects of strategy, war and seduction; and unaware of the Law of Attraction. The reason is that strategy-minded brainiacs have more in common with "God" than man; they know with absolute certainty that power was birthed by strategy, war and seduction; and the Law of Attraction is what made them successful in the first place. Therefore, if you ever see a "devoutly religious" mastermind, he or she is simply *posing* as religious for his or her benefit, and incorporating religion into grand strategy. If you ever see a mastermind publicly going out of his way to condemn or criticize the works of Sun Tzu, Machiavelli and Robert Greene, then, assuredly, in order to maintain advantage, he is misleading you to prevent you from understanding how he thinks. And, if you ever see a mastermind who seems oblivious to the Law of Attraction, he or she is playing dumb for a reason that you may never come to understand. The point is that mastermind psychology can never be understood by studying the psychological findings put forth by conventional psychologists—or unconventional psychologists who were not masterminds themselves. In response to this book, I may eventually do an in-depth study on mastermind psychology but, for now, if you seek to understand the mastermind psychology of Donald J. Trump, after reading this book, I suggest that you pay more attention to his words, behavior and political actions, and do so impartially but with a focus on strategy, seduction and power.

The contemporary, social concept of morality is skewed, and true political reasoning is what has turned Donald Trump into a modern-day Machiavelli. As a wise man once told me, "morality is primarily a religious issue," and the problem with America, although I love this country to death, is the fact that many of us are simply too fucking "religious." At least, that is what we say and how we present ourselves to the world. Our churches are wrought with sexual promiscuity, greed, pedophilia and extreme hypocrisy that many of us are aware of but still deny, due to a ridiculous hope that, eventually, things may change; the "Devil" is the cause of it all; and, one day, Jesus Christ "will come in the clouds with great power and glory" to put an end to all of our misery and strife. If morality is primarily a religious issue, then, we have no real religious model to use as a basis for morality. In actuality, true morality is dictated by one's inner self, and this is why so many people inside the Church resist the Biblical and Church-related tenets and conventions that they know go against their inner nature, whatever it is. Additionally, if there is really a "separation of church and state" in this country, then, why do certain people in the Church have political influence over others in the state, and vice-versa? In fact, the phrase "separation of church and state" does not even appear in the United States Constitution, but average, conditioned minds would beg to differ and dispute this until their lips fall off.

As for true political reasoning, it is not based on conventional, political ideology, because what most of us think we know about politics is so far from our political roots that it is ludicrous beyond definition. Politics concerns power, power is acquired via strategy and physical or mental warfare, and strategy demands use of the art of seduction. He or she who knows and fully understands this, therefore, knows and understands what true political reasoning is, and Donald Trump is definitely cognizant of this. It is utilized in his campaign. It is shown in his words, behavior and political actions. It flows through his entire *being*, and the only people who are unaware of this are those whose minds are still trapped in a box of conformism. As expected, numerous critics may not like what I am saying, but it is what it is, and the truth is the truth, whether they like it—or not.

The Age of the Cyclops

Lastly, "they" say that we are living in the "Age of Information," and that this is the most amazing era to be living in information-wise because, due to the rise of technology and the Internet, for the first time in human history, we have *tons* of information available at our fingertips that we can acquire with ease. To many people, this may sound amazing. But, ask yourself this question: "With all of this information available, why are so many people still so goddamned *dumb*?" How many times have you encountered someone who had access to the same information you had and thought they were right about something they truly believed they knew, but it turned out that they did not know a goddamned thing and were wrong on virtually all accounts? This seems to happen to me all the time. People think they know stuff, but do not know squat. They spend countless hours with mobile computers in their hands and are still uninformed when it comes to matters of reality, and this shows us just how ignorant many people in our society actually are, much more how preposterous it is to even consider the current era the "Information Age," when no one is really taking time out to *absorb* that information. Therefore, I have, in justifiable manner, decided to dub this modern age "The Age of the Cyclops." This is the only description that fits.

In Greek mythology, a Cyclops was a member of a savage race of one-eyed giants. These giants were said to be huge monsters with grotesque features who rose to power and lived brutal, debauched lives. However, they were great workers confined to the Underworld by their own father, Uranus, who was afraid that they would threaten his power. Eventually, though, they were freed by Zeus and the Olympians. There is more to the myth, of course, but this is just a quick overview. Now, fast forward to the modern era. People of the modern era consider a Cyclops an ignorant, uneducated person. Now, look at the parallels. Western ruling class scholars credit Greek culture as the source of Western civilization, and findings from countless studies suggest that America is one of the most uneducated countries on earth. And the United States is a "giant" superpower. Because of our military exploits and the varying degrees of damage that we have left in our path in countless countries overseas, many foreigners consider us a nation of savages, believing that, for us, brutality and debauchery are part of our way of life. However, when it comes to business, we are "good workers." In parallel, America itself seems to be a Cyclopian race, and the Social Matrix here is so powerful that most people will never wake up.

With someone like Donald Trump running for president, and him being as real and blunt as he is, one would think that most people who are tired of having corrupt politicians in office would support him. It seems, however, that most of these people are still trying to figure out what they want to do, and this indecision helped inspire me to write this book. The conditioned minds among us with no hope whatsoever will take the conventional route and vote for Hillary Clinton and, like old slaves, boast about the good deed they have done for their "master" at the ballot box. And, if she wins, the same political cycle will continue, eventually resulting in them regretting their decision *big* time. But those who want the truth will gravitate toward Trump, whether they agree with some of his notions and comments or not. The question remains: Why put a Cyclops in office when you can elect an ingenious Prince? Peasants make decisions based on emotions, but Princes and Princesses are guided by reason predicated on facts drawn from an understanding that we live in a *real* world, where conventionalism is anti-political. As Robert Greene states in his book, *Mastery*: "The conventional mind is passive—it consumes information and regurgitates it in familiar forms. The dimensional mind is active, transforming everything it digests into something new and original, creating instead of consuming." Trump's mind is definitely dimensional and, where power is concerned, all signs point to him being the better choice for America. We are now at a crucial point in which we have to choose between a Cyclopian bureaucrat and a pragmatic mastermind. Are you simply "for America," or are you "for America being *great* again"? I do not know about you, but I am inclined to choose the latter. In politics, it is *always* best to take the Machiavellian approach—not the conventional one.

3

Politics and The Art of Seduction: What the Public *Really* Wants

I n his much-acclaimed book *The Art of Seduction*, author Robert Greene sets the stage for his readers in the beginning by informing them about the true nature of seduction and its power. Throughout this book, I have been touching on the same here and there—but it is now time for us to get to the heart of the matter. Therefore, allow me to begin with an excerpt from Greene that backs something I have been saying all along in regard to seduction and politics, and just seduction in general. In the Preface, Greene says:

> *Today, no political campaign can work without seduction...*
> *It is pointless to try to argue against such power, to imagine*
> *that you are not interested in it, or that it is evil and ugly.*
> *The harder you try to resist the lure of seduction—as an*
> *idea, as a form of power—the more you will find yourself*
> *fascinated.*

If you are one of those people who believe that truth in the political arena is the primary winner of votes, you are sadly mistaken. Truth, or the illusion of it, is definitely an important political component, but most votes are won by *seduction*. This, however, is not a bad thing because, whether we know it or not, we all *want* to be seduced. We just want to be seduced the *right* way. Seduction is simply a part of life, and we have all seduced someone, for some reason, at some point in our lives. And, in many ways, women are the most skilled seducers of all. In fact, they are the ones who *created* seduction. However, over time, after being seduced for so long, men eventually caught on and started doing the same thing. As empires rose and fell, the use of brute force in power began to wane and was supplanted by strategy of the seductive nature, although there were indeed moments in which brute force was necessary in the squashing of enemies. But those who had no true power to call their own began to understand that the only way they could rise to power was to put themselves in a position to *acquire* it, which is where the art of seduction came in—and the rest is history. In politics, people went from seducing individuals to seducing the masses, and this became so common among politicians that it eventually turned into a way of life.

Now, enter the 21" Century. America is the new Greece, the new Rome, and more people are involved in the political process than ever before. Even though most politicians are not masterminds, if they know nothing else, they know that seduction of the masses is mandatory if they want to acquire the required number of votes that will put them in office. Thus, they seduce, knowing that, as Robert Greene says, "no political campaign can work without seduction." This is a *fact*. And the only people who denounce this truth are: (1) those who have been brainwashed to believe that seduction is malevolent, and (2) those who are skilled at it but downplay it in order to keep their seductive intentions unknown, for whatever reason(s). In relationships, we want our lovers to seduce us, because it makes us feel good. In entertainment culture, we seek the same. In war, we seduce the other side in order to win. In society, we seduce others to get what we want. And it is no different in politics. In life, humans seduce, and they want to *be* seduced. That is just basic psychology, and *anybody* can do it. As Robert Greene also says:

> *Seduction is a game of psychology, not beauty, and it is within the grasp of any person to become a master at the game. All that is required is that you look at the world differently, through the eyes of a seducer.*

When you begin to start thinking for yourself, instead of through the conventional lens of propriety, and you make the decision to start thinking like a seducer, virtually everything about your life will change. You will come to realize that most of the people you know and encounter are either already seducing you, or trying to do so, and this gives you the insight to decide whether or not you can use the seduction of others to your own benefit. You will experience a heightened perception of the world around you and take pleasure in playing the game. And, as for politics, this heightened perception will cause you to see through a lot of the bullshit tactics that politicians use in their efforts to seduce you the *wrong* way—Hillary Clinton included.

> *Seducers have a warrior's outlook on life… Seducers do not improvise; they do not leave this process to chance. Like any good general, they plan and strategize, aiming at the target's particular weaknesses.*

In America, as in the Roman Republic and Roman Empire, we love warriors, gladiators, fighters who do not take shit from *anybody*. We love our military, and we love our leaders when they have the balls to do what many of us do not have the courage to do, but still desire to see done. And Trump embodies this to a T. He has a warrior outlook on life that we are attracted to. He plans, strategizes, aims at his targets' weaknesses, wages war against them and *wins*. This is just who he is, and it seduces the hell out of us, because we know that, though heightened in the mass media, it is real. And, after years of seeing countless politicians' seductive power wane, it just feels good to see someone *real* running for office, although we may not agree with everything he says and does. Whether we are for or against him, Trump's dominance has many of us talking about him day and night, which proves that we have *already* been seduced. And we *like* it.

> *Finally, seducers are completely amoral in their approach to life… Knowing that the moralists, the crabbed repressed types who croak about the evils of the seducer, secretly envy their power, they do not concern themselves with other people's opinions… Get rid of any moralizing tendencies, adopt the seducer's playful philosophy, and you will find the rest of the process easy and natural.*

Most of us in society who know what we want out of life do not give a damn about other people's opinions, because we are going to do what we want to do regardless. Because we know this about ourselves, we naturally gravitate toward people like Trump who feel the same way that we do. If those among us who are overly concerned with morality begin to think like seducers, their concern with morality will fly out of the window, because seducers are too smart to let moralism hinder their success. And success, in some form, is what we all want. All of Trump's opponents who have tried to remain moral in their attacks against him have lost miserably, because they confined their attacks to a box of ridiculous notions. Trump, on the other hand, fought morality with strategic amorality and won, and even the holiest of us were attracted to his amoral stratagems. From this, the following question arises: If we are supposed to be moral and do not want to be seduced, then, why are we exhausting so much energy tuning in to see what an amoral man like Donald Trump is doing, while looking forward to whatever he is going to do next? Because we are caught up in his seduction—that is why. And we would not be caught up in it if we truly had no desire to be seduced.

One final point that I would like to make on this subject is that, even though a lot of Democrats are going around shitting on The Donald profusely, all of us—Democrats, Republicans *and* Independents—are the reason that he is so successful in the first place. Let me tell you why. First of all, after the Bush administration left the White House and Democrats went in, the Democratic Party became soft. They took too many boots off the ground, spent too much time trying to make peace with the peace-less via negotiation, and spent too much money on the wrong things. While all of this was taking place, the Republicans made themselves look bigoted and xenophobic by over-bashing Obama and over-condemning his foreign policy endeavors. They also made themselves seem devious, unprincipled and savage by sloppily and unsuccessfully plotting Obama's downfall, and over-competing for political positions within their party, which resulted in the infighting that divided them. As for the Independents, they simply spent too much time publicly bashing *both* parties. All of this created an environment of discontentedness that created the platform which gave rise to Donald Trump, a mastermind outsider with inside connections, who recognized that this was an opportunity for greatness, devised a master plan, seized the moment, and the rest is...well, you already know the story. We can all say whatever we want to say about Donald Trump, but we *gave* him this opportunity, and that is pure reality. Why hate him now?

As Greene points out in Appendix B of his work, "seduction is the ultimate form of power." And Donald Trump is a brilliant power player who is also masterful at matters of seduction, which most of us have seen with our own eyes. This makes him a formidable opponent, and America is in dire need of a formidable president. In spite of her countless years in politics, Hillary Clinton is just not on this man's level. On a scale of 1 to 10, her seduction power is probably 4 or 5; her power-playing skills, maybe a 5 or 6, while Trump is easily pulling 9 or 10 on both scales. Instead of looking at the results of polls conducted by organizations that are partial to a certain political party, I suggest that you look to *history* for guidance concerning who you should vote for in this upcoming election. Cleopatra would *laugh* at Hillary Clinton, but Machiavelli would *endorse* The Donald. Furthermore, Clinton has always been a third wheel in power, but Trump has always been *the* wheel. And, now, it is no different in politics. In addition, knowing that the masses *want* to be seduced, we have to ask ourselves the following question: "Of Hillary Clinton and Donald Trump, which one can we trust the most in matters of power and seduction?" Thus far, in power and politics, we have only seen Clinton playing second and third fiddle to her husband, Bill Clinton, Al Gore and President Obama. But we have seen Trump holding his own, while standing alone, since the beginning.

Abraham Lincoln once said: "You can fool all the people some of the time, and some of the people all the time, but you cannot fool all the people all the time." Are we going to continue getting hoodwinked by a false notion of morality that aims to nullify the power of seduction? Or will we make the right decision and use the power of seduction to help our country restore its greatness? Every mastermind I know would tell you that, throughout her career, Hillary Clinton has played an integral role in the brainwashing of Americans, not to mention the world. That she has, on occasion, deliberately kept us from the truth, and seduced us into believing a multitude of lies. This kind of seduction will *never* help America move forward. However, Trump's seduction is founded on greatness. Either go with the snake, or go with the lion. But, whatever you do, do not fall for the trap of Hillary's lying. And, with that said, I conclude.

4

America and the Art of War: Have We *Really* Forgotten?

Humans are hard-wired for warfare, and conflict is just a way of life. The notion of peace is an illusion, and those who subscribe to it are totally out of touch with reality. No matter how much we try to avoid conflict, like death, it will ultimately find us. The truth is that there will never be peace on earth, and we humans will fight among each other until the day we die. As Sun Tzu mentions in his treatise on warfare, "The art of war is of vital importance to the State...It is a matter of life and death, a road either to safety or to ruin. Hence it is a subject of inquiry which can on no account be neglected," and we need to come to grips with this reality. The "freedoms" that we enjoy so much come with a price, and it seems that many of us have forgotten this. The next time you see a wounded veteran, you need to remember that that veteran's sacrifice was *part* of this price. No freedom is ever accomplished without bloodshed, warfare and death. Therefore, when it comes to power, the art of war is an absolute necessity.

The same is true when it comes to politics, since it deals with the activities associated with the governance of a country or state, and conflict is common among individuals or parties having or hoping to achieve power. In government, presidents are the head, politicians constitute the body, and The People are meant to be the nation's spine. At one time, in spite of our conflict among one another domestically, we never really allowed our awareness of outside threats to be anything but keen. When our enemies went out of their way in their numerous attempts to destroy us, we put aside our petty squabbles, rallied together as a nation and crushed them, totally. Back then, where warfare was concerned, America was *strong*. The government, and the majority of The People, were on one accord. Politicians were ready for war, got the okay from The People, presidents rallied the troops, and it was on. Most of our foreign enemies simply knew not to fuck with the United States, and they avoided conflict with us as best they could. And, then, Obama hit the scene seemingly out of the blue, and America got soft. There is no doubt about it, in the beginning, he came out *hard*, like a general, and his campaign was one of the shrewdest I have ever seen. However, at some point in his first term, and especially the second, he turned out to be no different than any of the other politicians who have gotten away from America's political roots. His seeming desire to negotiate with enemies and issue sanctions rather than ass whooping turned a leviathan nation into a governmental joke, and an astounding number of people fell for his seduction, believing that "having a national conversation" would somehow engender change. He soft sold America, and we bought it. The art of war was superseded by the art of negotiation and irresolution, which failed us miserably. Old America died, and political warfare died with it.

"Political warfare" is the "aggressive use of political means to achieve national objectives." Conventional politicians, however, have been conditioned to believe that political warfare is the utilization of *all* national means, short of war, but *true* politicians are Machiavellian-minded and know that warfare, be it mental or physical, is an integral part of politics. The former political type has, in turn, conditioned a considerable number of The People to adopt their way of thinking, and this is also why America is so soft. But a strong nation can only go soft for so long, and now, with Trump's rise and Obama's imminent departure occurring simultaneously, and having witnessed the political deterioration of the state, The People are beginning to awaken and realize that it is now time to reclaim our political greatness. The only way for us to do this is to assume the Machiavellian mindset, which is why we *need* Trump, his influence and people like him to call the strategic shots that most of our "leaders" are too ignorant and afraid to call. This is the only way that we can pick up the political ball and bounce it on the heads of our adversaries as necessity requires in order to maintain the freedoms that our soldiers are living and dying for on behalf of our country.

Now, to the politicians among us who are in pursuit of power, I say unto you, if you truly aspire to attain power, scratch whatever you think you know about politics, get back to your Machiavellian roots, and play the game. Make *The Prince, The Art of War, The 48 Laws of Power, The Art of Seduction* and *The 33 Strategies of War* your political "bibles." Absorb their knowledge and abide by them as a devout Christian would the Holy Bible, and a devout Muslim, the Holy Quran. Let their tenets guide you. Accept the fact that conflict is a part of life and timidity will get you nowhere. Religious notions of piety are no substitute for stone cold reality, so scratch that, too. If you truly want power and consider yourself a "politician," you *have* to play the game. There can be no other way.

Have we really forgotten how America was founded in the first place? Removing racial sentiment and weak notions of morality from the equation, from the power perspective, let me tell you what *really* happened. A group of people fled their homeland to escape religious prosecution, and they ended up here, in the Americas, where another group of people had already been existing and ruling for thousands of years. However, Group One was in survival mode, looking for a new place to call home, and Group Two already had a home. The ultimate aim of Group One was domination and, after having already dominated, the ultimate aim of Group Two was harmony and goodwill. Group One had a Machiavellian mindset, and Group Two did not.

And, when the former group noticed this weakness, it used shrewd strategy and advanced weaponry to seize Group Two's land and call it its own, and the rest is history. Group One has been in power ever since. Such is the benefit of maintaining the Machiavellian mindset.

At the end of the day, Americans need to realize that power played at the Machiavellian level is the source of America's *existence*. If you deny this for any reason and take pride in criticizing your own country, say what you want about the United States, but keep it real. If you hate America that much, pack up your shit, hop on a plane and leave. But, I guarantee you, if true power is what you want, you definitely will not acquire it wherever you end up going.

At any rate, Donald Trump is the best bet that we have of restoring our nation to its former greatness, and helping it become the feared political juggernaut it used to be. A black woman I encountered a couple days ago, commenting on Trump, said to me: "Donald Trump must be crazy! What in the hell does he mean by saying, 'Make America *great* again?' When was America ever great?" The only thing I could do was shake my head and laugh, because it was apparent that she knew nothing about power, politics, strategy, Machiavelli or even Donald Trump, for that matter. She had never even heard of *The Prince* before talking to me, and it was obvious from some of her other comments that she views America through the lens of color. The very next day, while sitting in my SUV brainstorming, I encountered a white woman who engaged me in political discussion, after seeing a Donald Trump book on my dashboard. Although she *had* heard of Machiavelli and *The Prince*, she admitted that she had never studied him, and had never read any of his works. She has never read any of Donald Trump's books either, or taken time out to study him. However, she passionately made known to me her strong animosity toward Donald Trump. I asked her why she dislikes him so much, and this is what she said: "Because, as a woman, I just can't trust him." The more she talked, the more it became obvious to me just how much she perceives America through the eyes of gender.

Later that day, I ran across a man with only one arm. As with the others, he and I started conversing, mostly small talk at first, and the conversation eventually turned to politics. He said he was a veteran who served under both the Bush and Obama administrations before getting his arm blown off during the latter. He also told me that he did not care about losing his arm, because he sacrificed it on behalf of his country. Right then and there, my respect for him went through the roof. He spoke with passion, had the demeanor of a general and the mindset of a master strategist. And he was well-read, *The Prince* and Robert Greene's works included. Concerning power, he said, "Most Americans don't understand power, because they are too distracted by powerless pursuit. If they really knew the sacrifices we've made for them, they'd probably be scared to death." And, regarding Trump, he said, "Trump is a *genius*, man. Hell yeah, I'm voting for him! That would be like having Machiavelli himself in office." Of course, we talked about much more, but business called, and we went our separate ways. But I will never forget this man. Unlike the other two people I mentioned, he was politically aware and understood power at its deepest levels. More than anyone else, it was this man who gave me hope that, someday soon, my American brethren will awaken from conventional slumber and help make their country great again.

Lastly, while conducting research for this book, I saw a commercial in which the narrator stated the following: "In this generation, you have to be great at something before actually doing it." For the life of me, I cannot remember what kind of commercial it was, but the message definitely stood out to me. This statement is so true! The times have changed, and The People no longer have the patience to deal with leaders who are mediocre power players who are not already great at what they do. Now, more than ever, after being let down by politicians and presidents for so long, people want to see *results*. Apparently, the art of war is not of any significant interest to Hillary Clinton, nor has she ever been great at it at all. In fact, her war-related experience is so maladroit and far from shrewd that it is ridiculous. Quite a number of people in government say that she is responsible for making Libya a failed state, that she contributed to Honduras' downfall, and is to blame for the rise of ISIS, among other things. Not to mention that she has been accused of committing various war crimes. From this, it is obvious that war is not an *art* to her, and Machiavellian maneuvering, surely, is not her forte (google Zach Cartwright's *U.S. Uncut* article entitled "Hillary Clinton's War Crimes Are Unforgivable: No Real Progressive Could Ever Support Her").

However, Trump, on the other hand, in spite of having never been elected to public office, is an accomplished power player who takes the art of war seriously. People who are clueless about power, warfare and human psychology would probably argue that Trump's tactical maneuverability and success outside of politics mean nothing, because politics and big government constitute an entirely different world where power and war are drastically different from what he is used to. What they fail to realize, however, is that power is power, and it takes a certain kind of mindset to handle and utilize it accordingly—a mindset like Donald Trump's. This man is Machiavellian to the bone, many world leaders are *already* afraid of him, and he is virtually unstoppable. Since the beginning of his current run for president, more so than any of his political contenders, Trump has been, and still is, the *only* presidential candidate with the power, personality, personal wealth, influence and experience to make the United States Machiavellian again. This is what this country has traditionally been and is meant to be. Although many of us have forgotten this, *Donald Trump still remembers.* Give the man a chance and I guarantee that, where the art of war and the game of power are concerned, unless you are just blind to reality, you will *not* be disappointed—and, remember, Niccolò DaVinci told you this first.

5

The *Real* Power of the Law of Attraction: Only the *Hungriest* Will Survive

In 2006, Rhonda Byrne's now globally bestselling book, *The Secret*, was published, and the world as we know it was forever changed, for the better. The theme of her book was what is now widely known as the Law of Attraction, the belief that we attract to ourselves whatever it is we think about, whether good or bad. From my own experience, the experiences of others, as well as my studies on world history, I have come to know with absolute *certainty* that the Law of Attraction is not just a philosophy or belief, but rather a *Universal Truth* that could *never* be empirically denied. It is as real as real can be. Prior to *The Secret*, there were many other authors, speakers and television writers and producers talking about the same subject, but something about Byrne's work on the topic stood out to people the most. This "something" was simply the strength of her willpower and desire to get her message out to the world. And, ever since, millions and millions of people have been discussing and practicing the Law of Attraction—and those who have been practicing it the most have been accomplishing the so-called "impossible." And, guess what   Donald J. Trump is part of this group.

No matter who you are, what "race" you happen to be a part of, what country you live in, what you have or *do not* have, who you know or *do not* know or what hardships you have experienced in your life, you can *rise*. Whatever it is that you want, if you bring yourself to see and want it badly enough, no matter what it is, you can *have* it, you can *be* it, and eventually, as Bob Proctor would probably say, you will be able to "hold it in your hand." The problem with a lot of people, however, is that, when it comes to the things that they *say* they want, they simply do not think big enough, and do not believe with all their might that they can get it. And this is why they fail. In life, in business, in politics—it is all the same. It you do not already have the life that you want, or if you are not getting extremely *close* to having it, then, you are simply not thinking BIG enough. This is stone-cold reality. This is 2016, and there is no excuse whatsoever that can justify why one is not thinking BIG, especially if you are living here in the United States. If you are not successful or almost getting there, the only person responsible for your failure is YOU. And every successful person I know would tell you the same thing.

The real power of the Law of Attraction lies in the strength and depth of your *hunger*. In terms of success, that old saying, "Only the strong survive," is some of the dumbest shit I have ever heard, and let me tell you why. Although it mostly holds true concerning Darwin's theory of natural selection, as well as typical brutish competition among men (and women, too, for that matter), when it comes to success, strength does not necessarily *guarantee* accomplishment. One can be as strong in the mind as one can be, but if that person is not *hungry* enough, strength alone will do him or her no good. The other problem with this saying is the word "only." If *only* the strong survive, then, why do we see so many strong people being outdone by the so-called "weak"?

For example, although many people agree that President Obama has been weak from the beginning, he still outmaneuvered the strong back in 2008 and won the election in a landslide. Take Kanye West as another example. Before he acquired celebrity status and rose to the top in Hip Hop, the world knew nothing about him. He went to art school, attended college but dropped out, and even worked at The Gap. But he was always engaged in music. And, then, years later, he popped up on the Hip Hop scene as a producer on Jay-Z's *Blueprint* album and, eventually, began working tirelessly on his own album, *The College Dropout*. However, because he was completely different from the typical cluster of rappers who were confined to a box, he faced difficulty being accepted as a rapper in his own right by figures in the music industry. Because of his aforementioned background, people doubted him, perceived him as "soft," tried to shit on him for not being "gangsta" enough, said he was weak, and even perceived him as being gay. They had never imagined, in a thousand years, that this supposedly "weak" entertainer would someday surpass the "strong" in Hip Hop and attain wealth and undeniable, iconic status in Hip Hop and entertainment. Then, his debut studio album dropped, was certified *platinum* and, now, he is one of the most controversial and awarded Hip Hop artists of all time. If he was so "weak," then, how did he surpass the strong and become who he is today?

This "only the strong survive," "survival of the fittest" shit holds no weight when it comes to the Law of Attraction, unless strength is pushed by desire, because strength alone does not attract *anything*—but a person's hunger or desire does. At the end of the day, it is all about who hungers for something the most, and it does not matter if you are weak or strong. When it all boils down to it, Obama became president because his desire to *be* president was more *intense* than all of his competitors' desires to become the same—and the same is true regarding Kanye West. We are currently seeing the same thing happen with Donald Trump. In fact, if Trump had decided to run for president back in 2008, with the same hunger that he has now, there would not even *be* a President Obama.

Extraordinarily BIG thinking, backed by extremely INTENSE desire, is what has made Donald Trump a billionaire in the first place. And it is the same thing that pushed him from Trump Tower to the White House. Because he has not yet been officially elected president, predictably, most critics who read this will wonder what the hell I mean when they see the words "pushed him from Trump Tower to the White House," because Obama, not Trump, is *already* in the White House. This is because most critics suffer from what I call "Limception Virus," that is, the disease of limited perception. What many of them, and just people in general, fail to remember is that, aside from the fact that Trump is already *friends* with the Clintons outside of politics, Trump has already *been* inside of the White House, and his imprint is still there.

After Trump's involvement in the Birther Movement resulted in the public disclosure of Obama's long-form birth certificate in 2011, Trump attended the White House Correspondents' Dinner, to which he was invited. While there, however, "Saturday Night Live" comedian Seth Meyers, and even President Obama himself, seemed to go out of their way to *shit* on The Donald by making him the butt of what many people would call some very disrespectful jokes—all for the entire world to see. Obama shitted on his "credentials and breadth of experience," and Meyers shitted on his prior run for president by calling it a "joke," somewhat alluding that Trump could *never* be president. And, while sitting in the audience, Trump seemed *pissed* (google the 2011 White House Correspondents' Dinner video and check it out yourself), although he later stated that he was not affected at all by any of this, and he could have been telling the truth. But one thing I do know, above all else, is this: history has proven time and time again that, when extraordinarily BIG thinkers are shitted on, especially when they are shitted on in front of *everybody*, they do not get mad—they get *motivated* and, then, they get *even*. Although only Trump himself knows exactly what and how he felt in that moment, I personally believe that what transpired at this dinner motivated The Donald to think even bigger than he usually thinks about politics, to go even harder than he normally does, and to do the impossible by either becoming president or coming so close to winning the election that his power, credentials and "breadth of experience" could go down in history in a *huge* way and *never* be denied. And, look at him now, at the top of his game in politics. He did not become the Republican presidential nominee through sheer strength alone—the intensity of his desire, and the enormity of his thoughts, got him there. If *he* can do it, just imagine what YOU can do!

Now, think about all of Trump's political opponents who competed against him during the Republican primaries. If the Law of Attraction were not real, and chance or luck, or a particular "God," decides who will be successful or not, then, this means that any one of them could have defeated Trump at any time. And it is possible that at least a few of them prayed to "God," asking him to give them the power to defeat The Donald, but that shit did not work either. See, words and thoughts have *power*, and this power shapes one's world by way of attraction. Trump's opponents were focused more on trying to beat him than trying to become president. Their minds were locked in a state of competition, but over-concern with competition is a negative vibration that only attracts negativity and failure. Trump, on the other hand, *knew* he would beat them, so, his mind was *not* locked in competition at all. And his confidence, which is a *positive* vibration, attracted victory and success. He wanted to be president more than he wanted to beat them, because he already *knew* that they were no match for him, and this is why they all dropped like flies before him. They were just thinking too small, so they lost.

If you truly want to be successful in politics, or otherwise, do not make the same mistake that these people did. You have to *be* hungry and *stay* hungry; *see* and *feel* yourself having what you want before you even acquire it; absolutely *refuse* to think small; *avoid* thoughts and words that cause negative vibrations; *never* see yourself in competition with *anybody*; have *supreme* confidence in yourself and your abilities; *keep* your mind focused on the *prize*; and, then, go for the *gusto!* This is the *only* way that you will ever become and be what and who you want to be.

This is no laughing matter. If you truly want something out of life, you have to *go hard* for that shit, like Mike Tyson went hard to become a *champion.* Oh, and, if you do not know, last I checked, Tyson himself is still a supporter of Donald Trump. He is also a wise, intelligent genius *in real life*, and I am willing to bet that he would agree with what I have just told you about success.

A final point that I would like to make in regard to success is that, while in pursuit of *anything* big, you will, inevitably, encounter "haters" who, for whatever reason, seem to make it their life mission to try to sabotage your success. And these people will come out of the woodwork, in *many* forms, in their efforts to try to stop you. Random people who you do not even know; acquaintances with whom you are on "good terms"; people that you have been friends with for quite some time; relatives, including some in your immediate family; and even significant others, *including your spouse*—at some point, in some way, unless they are *really* real, will try to stop you from accomplishing your dream. Most of it will be due to envy, jealousy and/or revenge for something you did, or did not do, that offended them. But some people just seem to be *wired* this way. They are just *born* haters, so, no matter *what* you do, they are going to hate on you regardless. And, sometimes, you will find yourself frustrated when having to deal with them, which will result in you cutting off, or simply avoiding, a lot of people who do not mean you any good at all. At times, you will want to crush them into the ground for fucking with you, and that is understandable. However, when you encounter people like this, the best way to deal with them is to *crush them with your success.* By doing so, you will make them miserable for the rest of their lives, and that is the best revenge you could ever inflict upon a person—lifetime misery. So, when haters come, and they surely will, *do not* let them distract you, ever. Unless they pose a *serious* threat to you, your family and/or your livelihood, do not even *think* about them. And, if ever they *do* pose such a threat, be patient and, when the time is right, *crush them totally for real*, however you decide to interpret that. If you do this, for the most part, you will not really have any problems at all. What others may consider problems for you will mean *nothing*, because you will be too *focused* to have problems.

If you truly want power, you have to take the advice in this chapter and put it to use. And this is not me being arrogant or a know-it-all—this is just reality. Donald Trump already knows this, and this is why he is so wealthy and successful. You say that you want to succeed, right? You also agree that you are a BIG thinker, huh? You believe with all of your heart that you can accomplish whatever it is you put your mind to. Am I right? Well, *prove* your haters wrong! *Do* it! Do your thing! If they do not like it, *fuck* them (not literally, of course—unless you *want* to)! And I said that with pun intended. You were not born to be mediocre. Do not let anything or anybody stop you! Get *hungry*. Become *hungrier*. Then, become the *hungriest*. When you do this, hell with the *sky* being the limit—there will *be* no limit to how high you can rise, how far you can go. Make *magic*. Do the "impossible." Spark controversy. Give the critics something to talk about, with their dumb asses. This is all you have to do. This is YOUR time, YOUR age, YOUR epoch, YOUR era! And, with that said, like Jay-Z (who some believe secretly supports Donald Trump) would probably say: "On to the next one!"

6

Only Knowledge Applied *Shrewdly* Equals Power: III-Wisdom of the Ages

In retrospect, throughout life, how many times have you heard the old saying, "Knowledge is power"? Most likely, more times than you can imagine. However, ask yourself the following question: "If power is so easily acquired through knowledge, then, why are so many knowledgeable people so powerless?" Right now, I can name a *million* knowledgeable people I either know or have met personally, but only a tiny majority of them are powerful in some major way that really matters. When this was first told to me in my youth, I actually believed it. However, it did not take long for me to realize how ridiculously impractical it was because, the second time someone told this to me, I instantly realized that both of the individuals who dropped this so-called "jewel" on me were the epitome of powerless. They were "smart" as hell, in the book-related sense, but were poor, even though they both had degrees and decent jobs. So, just me being me, I asked them, "If you have all of this knowledge, then, where is your power?" And, I swear, they both told me the *exact* same thing: "The power is in the *mind*." All I could do was shake my head and laugh at how seriously ill-advised they were about power, because life had already taught me that true power lies in the ability to control and influence people, things, events, etc. And this ability, first and foremost, comes from *shrewd* application of acquired knowledge. Therefore, if one truly wants to attain power, especially politically, it is absolutely *ridiculous* to accept and adopt such an impractical notion.

We live in a world where the term "conventional wisdom" is synonymous with "common sense." However, because conventionalism is predicated on mass conformism, and the basis of common sense is practicality, wisdom, in the conventional sense, could never be grounded in reality. And there is a distinction between these two terms that makes this clear.

While recently online, I ran across a *WordPress.com* article by Kevin Kervick entitled "Conventional Wisdom vs. Common Sense" and, in this article, as its title makes clear, Kervick points out the difference between conventional wisdom and common sense, as defined by Wikipedia. Here is what he says:

> *While these terms are often used as synonyms, there is actually a substantial and important distinction to be made between them. According to Wikipedia:*
>
> *Conventional wisdom is a term used to describe ideas or explanations that are generally accepted as true by the public or by experts in a field.*
>
> *Common sense is the basic level of practical knowledge and judgment that we all need to help us live in a reasonable and safe way.*

As you can see, by definition, conventional wisdom is based on general public opinion, while common sense is centered on reality. I also ran across a *U.S.News.com* article by Kenneth T. Walsh entitled "A New Day for Politics: The 2016 Election Has Undermined All Conventional Wisdom" and, in this article, Walsh quotes Republican pollster, Frank Luntz, who stated:

> *There's no more normal. The new normal is no normal. Everything we expected has proven to be untrue....People feel betrayed.*

Additionally, Walsh himself states:

> *Many political leaders and analysts didn't see this coming, and the conventional wisdom that Trump would be a flash in the pan turned out to be embarrassingly wrong.*

Both of these statements are true. If age-old, conventional wisdom is based on common sense, then, why is common sense so commonly wrong? The reason many political leaders and analysts did not foresee Trump's political ascendance is that they were too caught up in normality to even expect anything else. They underestimated The People's discontent, and Trump, understanding the true nature of things, shrewdly applied knowledge that resulted in him acquiring political power.

In January, Karen Tumulty and Jenna Johnson published an article in *The Washington Post* entitled, "Why Trump May Be Winning the War on 'Political Correctness'" and, in this piece, they make some incredible points about why Donald Trump's crusade against political correctness seems to be winning. But, in my opinion, the most important point that they made lies in the following excerpt:

> *The Republican front-runner is "saying what a lot of Americans are thinking but are afraid to say because they don't think that it's politically correct," she said. "But we're tired of just standing back and letting everyone else dictate what we're supposed to think and do."*
>
> *In the 2016 Republican presidential primary season, "political correctness" has become the all-purpose enemy. The candidates have suggested that it is the explanation for seemingly every threat that confronts the country: terrorism, illegal immigration, an economic recovery that is leaving many behind, to name just a few.*

This article, like countless others, evidences how political correctness has contaminated modern American politics to such a level that use of it in the political arena drastically limits opportunities for politicians. It has simply gone too far, and this is why so many people are gravitating toward Trump. When I discovered, back in 2007, that politically correct leaders in Australia tried to ban Santa Clauses from saying, "ho, ho, ho," because the word "ho" informally references prostitutes and could be used derogatorily toward women, I knew then just how ridiculous political correctness was. Now, here in America, it is even worse, and the main reason most of our politicians are failing is that political correctness and worn-out, political strategies simply inhibit their power. Practical, commonsense-minded power pursuers connect with large numbers of people easily, because they actually understand The People. They are also able to keep their heads in the game because they never lose sight of reality. Contrarily, those who are politically correct-minded get outmaneuvered and *lose* supporters. The ill-gotten "wisdom" of old has taken modern political thought out of its element and, in Chapter 1, I touched on this in reference to the "12 Rules of Modern Politics" discussed by Nancy Benac in a related article. Let us briefly revisit these "12 Rules" in support of my point about worn-out strategy and political correctness.

The "12 Rules of Modern Politics"

1. Use Political Correctness When Speaking
2. Use Traditional Fundraising for Your Campaign
3. Use Surveys to Conduct Poll Testing
4. Be Consistent at All Times
5. Use Five-Point Policy Plans
6. Refrain from Using Vulgarity During Speeches
7. Rely On Super PACs
8. Avoid Appearing Monetarily Greedy
9. Do Not Insult People
10. Do Not Pick Fights
11. Be "Presidential"
12. Stay Groomed

The idiocy behind these so-called "rules" is the primary cause of political failure when strategy is confined to such politically correct ideology. True power cannot be gained by anyone following these politically ill guidelines, and absolute defiance of them is what made Trump the Republican nominee, *period*. Many people agree that he has *deliberately* broken all of these rules and, instead of hindering his power, his defiance only created *more* power. But it was not Trump's defiance itself that put him on top—it was the *shrewdness* behind it.

A final point I would like to make concerns an old saying that is so popular in politics it has fostered a standard way of thinking regarding upward mobility here in America. Since its coining, many politically correct politicians have quoted it. Now, it is basically taken as reality by most people who hear it. You yourself have probably heard it a million times, as people tried to convince you that "it's not *what* you know, it's *who* you know." But let us really examine this. How many people have you met over the years who claimed to know or have met powerful, famous or successful people, but are *not* powerful, famous or successful themselves? This happens to me all the time. Power, fame and success are oftentimes a *choice*, not a guarantee just because one may rub shoulders with such people at some point in life. In business, politics and life in general, countless people who have absolutely *no* connections to anybody who is somebody still become successful at what they do, and this fact puts this old maxim to shame. The problem with this mindset is that it causes people to doubt those who have all the essential qualities needed for power and success, simply because "they don't know people," and this does our country a huge disservice. At the end of the day, it is not what or who you know, but rather what you do or do *not* do, that determines whether you will be successful or powerful or not.

And this is a fact. Where Trump is concerned, although he definitely knew a lot of powerful people before he decided to run for president, what he *did* is more important and is the *true* cause of his success.

So, what did he *do*, exactly? Well, first and foremost, the first thing he did was set the stage for success by *choosing* to be successful. After making that decision, he did everything he was supposed to do to bring his dreams to fruition, and success came. Then, when the opportunity presented itself, he ran for president and did it in a grand way based on grand strategy. The people he knew prior to this did not make him the Republican presidential nominee. This accomplishment came as a result of what *The People* did—they believed in him and went out to vote. So, the belief that success is based on who one knows is the epitome of ignorance. Who we know may play a certain role in our success but, if we do not *do* something that resonates with them and mobilizes them in support of our cause, then, who they are does not even matter. This is reality.

By observing Trump without bias and close-mindedness, any person who is hell-bent on acquiring power, or maintaining it, can see the superiority of the Donald's strategy and accept that it works. Knowledge alone is *not* power; political correctness is *not* in tune with reality; "conventional wisdom" is nothing more than mass stupidity; and the ill wisdom of the ages that we defend so much, in many ways, is the cause of America's instability. Unless knowledge is taken to the next level via craftiness, true power can *never* be attained. Therefore, if ever America is to be made great again, Americans have to *do* something. And the main thing they need to do is take their *minds* back. If not, the cycle of ignorance will continue, the political arena will become an uber-hub of small thinking, and The People will never have a chance, as they do now, to elect an already powerful leader who is gifted at applying knowledge shrewdly.

Ill-wisdom of the ages has *no* place in modern politics and, if we truly want to see America become great again, we have to start thinking for ourselves. I guess the *real* question is this: Were you born to be politically correct, or were you born to be YOU? I believe that you know the answer. The only thing you have to do now is make the right decision. If you are smart enough to read between the lines of the modern, democratic establishment, then, I trust that you will.

7

Assassination and the Illuminati: Where *Trump* Fits into the Equation

For centuries, we have been hearing stories about what many believe is one of the most powerful, secret and controversial organizations in the world. In fact, it is often said to be *the* most powerful "secret society" on earth. From all of the knowledge that I have acquired over the years, and the people that I have come across, I can say with absolute certainty that this "society" or organization is *definitely* real. However, all conspiracy theories aside, from what I know, and *whom* I know for that matter, and based on things that I have done throughout my "travels," I can also attest that the Illuminati is not what a lot of people think it is. Human psychology teaches us that people generally fear what they do not understand, and the secrecy in which the Illuminati is shrouded is the main cause of conspiracy theories surrounding this clandestine society. The vast majority of its members are rich and powerful, yes. And strict confidentiality is woven into its fabric—I know. But does this mean that, as so many conspiracy theorists claim, the entire world is being dictated by the Illuminati? And, more specifically, do the ruling members of this society handpick people like Bill and Hillary Clinton, George Bush Jr. and Sr., Barack Obama and, now, Donald J. Trump to be president of the United States? As attention-grabbing as such a claim could be in theoretical circles, in *real* life, my friend, the answer is "No." Nevertheless, many people are convinced of the opposite.

"They" say that Obama is an Illuminati puppet, as well as the Antichrist, in the flesh. When it comes to Trump, however, the top two claims that I have been hearing and reading about allege one or two things: That (1) Trump is simply a *member* of the Illuminati, or (2) a target marked for *death* by the Illuminati because, supposedly, he has threatened to reveal "Illuminati secrets" if elected to the presidency. And all of this talk about Trump and the Illuminati has compelled me to write about this and clear it up, from a *practical* perspective that virtually anyone can understand. Hence, this chapter. I believe that it is very important for us humans, not just we Americans, to realize that there is *no* force outside of the self, powerful or not, that can control the human will. A certain level of mental conditioning or brainwashing can definitely control a mind, but only for a certain amount of time, if not seriously consistent, because the human mind, like Mother Nature, is too unpredictable. Eventually, it wakes up and returns to its senses. If everyone is being controlled by the Illuminati, then, why are millions of freethinking people thinking for themselves? If one could only acquire riches through Illuminati approval, then, why are so many people getting rich, many of whom do not even believe in the Illuminati? And, if Donald Trump is "marked for death" by the "Illuminated Ones," as close as he is to possibly becoming president, why is he not dead yet? The majority of these claims are ridiculous, and I want you to see this for yourself. All you have to do is go to YouTube!

Here is an amusing activity in which I would like you to participate. Wherever you are right now, if you have access to the Internet, go to your Internet browser and visit YouTube's official website. When you are taken to the main page, type the following words into the "Search" box: "Donald Trump Illuminati." By the time you are even done typing it in, several related suggestions based on popular searches should pop up. You will see suggestions such as "Donald Trump Illuminati Confirmed," "Donald Trump Illuminati Exposed," "Donald Trump Illuminati 2016," "Donald Trump Illuminati Puppet," "Donald Trump Illuminati Card Game," and even "Donald Trump Illuminati Song." However, the first selection should simply read "Donald Trump Illuminati," the one you just typed in. Well, click on that first search suggestion. After doing so, you will be taken to a host of Illuminati-related, Donald Trump videos. Most of them are whacky, but some have serious tones, and millions of people are actually *believing* this stuff. Just take a look at some of these videos, and you will see for yourself how ridiculous this notion of Donald Trump's supposed Illuminati membership truly is. But, most importantly, pay attention to the number of *views* each video has, because these views reflect the minds of The People.

My personal favorite, which makes me laugh uncontrollably at its nonsense, is a video entitled "Donald Trump Is Illuminati," uploaded by someone who calls himself, or herself, Peladophobian, whatever the hell that means. I will not say much about it but, if you have any semblance of a sense of humor, it will make you laugh. On a more serious note, though, I have found four YouTube videos about Trump and the Illuminati regarding his alleged membership and the purported Trump assassination to come, all of which I would like you to take a look at, if only briefly. Collectively, as of this writing, they have received 1,394,078 views. Here are their titles.

1. "Is Donald Trump the Illuminati's #1 Target for 2016? Says He'll Reveal 9/11 Conspiracy as President," by C. Ervana.
2. "Donald Trump Is a Member of the Illuminati—Video Proof!" by David Vose.
3. "Illuminati Planning Trump Assassination Attempt?" by Susan Duclos.
4. "Donald Trump Exposes the Illuminati 100% Real! Must See!!!" by Corporate America.

As you watch them, do so with an open mind. And, when I say "open," I mean *objectively*. Among other things, these videos talk about Trump threatening to expose who really knocked down the "Two Towers," Trump's alleged use of symbolic Illuminati hand shapes, JFK's "cryptic" speech about secret societies, and Trump's donations to politicians in return for favors. But here are some interesting things to point out. Concerning Trump's comments about the attack on the World Trade Center in 2001, in these videos, Trump is never seen or heard saying that *he himself* will reveal the truth about who really destroyed the Towers. He just says that it was not the Iraqis, and the "War On Iraq" was a "big, fat mistake" because there were never any weapons of mass destruction to begin with, and the government was fully aware of this, but lied about it to the public. The hand shapes are not just Illuminati symbols, but also hand signs that have become extremely popular in America's entertainment culture, thanks to celebrities. In the clips from JFK's "cryptic" speech, Kennedy *could have* been talking about the

Illuminati. But who is to say that he was not just referring to big-headed politicians who let power go to their heads? And Trump's generosity in business is no secret. The man understands human psychology. *Everybody* needs money so, when you give it to them, they help you when you need them to. In this regard, politicians are no different than most pastors inside of the Church. The Trump-Illuminati claim would sound much better if Trump *only* gave to politicians who are believed to be Illuminati members, but that is not the case. If Donald Trump were really an Illuminati initiate, as gifted as he is in shrewdness and showmanship, surely, by now, he would have said so himself without actually saying it, and done it in a way that made it *super* simple to read between the lines. As of yet, however, to my knowledge, he has not done so. Therefore, let me explain to you what it really going on.

As I mentioned earlier, people simply fear what they do not understand. If they do not fear it, the fact of not knowing just makes them *curious* about what is going on. And too much curiosity turns into suspicion, which eventually turns into theoretical speculation. This is just a matter of life. Masterminds are all around us, but the majority of people on the planet do not take time out to develop themselves into masterminds. All we see around us is the status quo. So, when someone who is different suddenly pops up, is unconventionally skilled in areas where most of us lack, and this person surpasses not only us but also our leaders, our natural tendency is to wonder who in the hell they are, where in the hell they came from, and how in the hell did they do it. We overanalyze things and eventually come to the conclusion that this person *has* to be connected to some "special" person or group. That is just how we humans are. Therefore, when Trump came along and did the so-called "impossible" by breaking record after record after record, the conspiracy theorists among us concluded that his rise could only be attributed to some kind of secret society. He was already rich and powerful when he entered the political arena and, since the Illuminati consists of mostly those who are rich and powerful, he *has* to be a member of the Illuminati. This is how we think when we are overly curious.

When it comes to Donald Trump and Illuminati membership, though you may have a different view, I just do not believe it. And I also do not believe that he is a target for Illuminati assassination. If we ask ourselves, "Regarding Illuminati membership and assassination, where does *Trump* fit into the equation?" the politically correct answer is, "We don't know." The definitive, commonsense answer, however, is "Nowhere." His rise in politics has nothing to do with secret society membership. Rather, it is the result of grand strategy. Period. If you are too close-minded to see this, then, if Hillary is elected, a few years from now, you will have a rude awakening. You may not be wise enough to see it now but, eventually, you will—believe me.

Last, but not least, conspiracy theorists generally have a tendency to believe that those who support alleged Illuminati members must be secret society members as well. Therefore, it would not surprise me to wake up someday and see the name "Niccolò DaVinci" wrapped up in some kind of Illuminati-based conspiracy theory. If ever you see such, *do not* believe it. After all, why would the Illuminati choose *me*, of all people? I am simply a writer exposing truth in an effort to awaken the somnambulant ones among us, for the betterment of my country. And there is *no* connection between the Illuminati and me that could ever be discovered, because one simply does not exist, although I do consider myself "Illuminated." A lot of these Illuminati theories are pure nonsense, and Donald Trump's rise is, undeniably, the result of shrewd, mastermind strategy. Even if he were selected by such an esteemed society for initiation, this would be more of an honor than a curse, because it would prove how much the elites respect his mind. In this respect, contrary to popular belief, for the powerful, joining the Illuminati is actually a *good* thing. Besides, if you yourself were a mastermind, would you rather surround yourself with a group of small-thinking individuals who have no power at all, or would you prefer to join a group of powerful elites who can increase your power and wealth for decades to come, even if you may have to sacrifice a few ignorant people along the way? Be honest with yourself. If logic does not make you lean toward the latter, this only evidences that your mind is not equipped for power.

The point is: If you are awaiting Trump's assassination, then, you have no idea how cunning and powerful he truly is. The more you anticipate his demise, the more he will succeed, and the higher he will rise. My advice to you: leave the conspiracy theories alone and focus on *reality*. In this day and age, that is the *only* way that you will be able to understand politics. But you do not have to take my word for it. Just keep your eyes on Trump, and commonsense will teach you otherwise. If not, though sad to say, there is merely no hope for you whatsoever. Power is not for you. It never *has* been. It never *will* be. Period.

8

A Wake-up Call for America: Revision of the Political Dynamic

The biggest mistake that many of us make in business and life, but especially in politics, is following popular methods that eventually burn out and stop working. If someone accomplishes something one way, instead of devising our own way of reaching that same goal, in our pursuit of whatever it is that we want, we relegate ourselves to the same methodology. But only a few of us actually become successful that way and, even in these cases, upon closer inspection, we find that, somehow and in some way, we end up throwing our own creativity in the mix, not sticking to the other person's plan *exactly*. The reason for this is that, inherently, we all know that, no matter what we are doing and how successful someone else has become at it, there is *always* room for improvement. The times are constantly changing, so our methods have to change with them in order for us to keep up and remain relevant. Even the writers of the Holy Bible understood this, which resulted in the writing of the New Testament, a new section for a new generation of believers. In politics, the same should apply. Donald Trump's success is showing us how the old political dynamic has lost most of its power, and I believe that this is a wake-up call for America.

I recently read an article in *The Denver Post* entitled, "Unchanging Donald Trump Creates a Changing Political World," and it makes clear just how much of an effect The Donald has had on modern politics since his rise to the top of not just the Republican Party, but also politics in general. This article talks about how Trump has made it clear that he is "not changing" and the rest of the political world is having to adjust to how *he* plays the political game. It asserts that the remainder of the 2016 political campaign season is likely to be fought on his terms, and also talks about how he "continually defies predictions" and forces his adversaries to adopt his tactics. As soon as I delved into this article, without question, because of what I already *know* about what is currently happening, and what is to come in modern politics, I agreed wholeheartedly with this piece.

But here is the thing: It is not just because of Donald Trump that politics is changing—it is because, as I have said before, this is what *The People* want. Like a married individual with a miserable, extreme baggage-carrying, spiteful, vindictive, small-thinking spouse, too many Americans are fed up with how things have been being run inside of the political establishment, especially under the Democrats. They want change because they have not been getting it. They want to see the game played by a different set of rules that is more in tune with reality and *true* political principles, which many of them have not even seen in their lifetime but read about in history books. They do not trust the government, they hate political correctness, they do not give a damn about polling if a candidate can do the job, and they know, hands down, that it is time for something and someone "different." Thus, knowing this, and with Trump on the scene embodying all of this, I mean, what did critics *think* was going to happen? For too long, the Establishment was not handling its business, and this created an anti-government, political revolution. The People are too involved now to relent anytime soon. It is what it is.

Political dynamics deal with the interplay between political leaders and voters, and the "endogenous and exogenous factors that impact the perceptions and goals of the electorate." But the bond between voters and their political leaders has been broken for a very long time. Voters used to be uncertain about whether they could trust politicians—now the majority of them *know* that they cannot trust them. And the internal and external factors that impact the perceptions and goals of the electorate are all but unknown to the average voter. Politicians have an obligation to share this information with the public, but they do not, and, if they do, they only provide watered-down information that serves their own best interests. But, now, with the new political revolution in full swing, The People are educating themselves, becoming more involved in politics, and doing so with the intention of engendering change. After witnessing

Trump's success, many of them are *beyond* inspired—they now *know* that, via the Machiavellian approach, they, too, can rise to power. And, guess what: they are coming to blow old political dynamics out of the water. It may take some of them months, and others years, but they are *definitely* coming, because they know it is time for change. Let me tell you a little more about this, to be specific.

In both the near and distant future, from The People will rise a dominant cluster of Machiavellian-minded politicians—from all races, ethnicities, genders, socioeconomic backgrounds, religions, etc.—who are hell-bent on acquiring power. And they will succeed, significantly. Some of them will be even more controversial than Donald Trump. For them, independent funding and free media exposure will come easily. Political correctness will have no power over their tongues; they will hugely defy polling and other predictions; play very dirty when they have to; and be "presidential" in their *own* ways. The voters will stand behind them; the highest of offices will elect them; they will stand up for what they believe in; and they will be completely loyal to The People. Some of them will be Democrats, but the majority of them, for quite some time, will be Republicans—and this will give rise to what I now call the "Political Renaissance." America will prosper, become virtually debt-free and, its citizens, many of them for the first time ever, will *truly* understand the meaning of "life, liberty and the pursuit of happiness," because they will be *living* it. Critics may call this a "prediction," but I call it "a pre-determined fact that will, eventually, become an inevitable reality." And the origin of it will point right back to Donald Trump, a Machiavellian mastermind who planted bounteous seeds that morphed into a Political Renaissance. America will truly be *great* again!

Democrats may scoff at the above assertion, but the incipient stages have already begun, with evidence of it right there in their own party. Said evidence is seen in the record numbers of Democrats who have been leaving the Democratic Party to join Trump on his journey to make America the great nation it used to be—and then make it better. The numbers are skewed in media reports, but those numbers are *definitely* large, because people are not as stupid as so many politicians think they are. If she were still alive, even Helen Keller would see that Trump is more trustworthy than Hillary is, and would make a better president than her any day. And there are many more Democrats out there who want to join Trump's team, but are too fearful to go because of groupthink and a sense of loyalty. However, sometimes, loyalty can be misguided. If you are a Democrat, only *you* know what is best for you. If your gut is telling you to vote for Trump, then, to hell with all of that groupthink, loyalty-to-a-broken-party shit. When you know what you know and feel what you feel, then, vote for whomever you really want to vote for. If the members of your party love you so much, they should respect your decision and let you go wherever you feel and believe you need to be. Besides, it is not like you cannot return to your old party later, because you can. But it is all about what is best for the *country*, and what *you* want— not them. So, make your *own* decisions, and never let anyone else think for you. That is not why you were put here on earth. You were born to do BIG things and, if you believe that you can help America do the same, then, you know what it is that you have to do. and you are not obligated to tell anybody anything. When it is time to cast your vote, you will know what to do.

Even Africans Americans who have been Democrats for years, some even decades, are leaving the Democratic Party to join Trump. I have personally talked to quite a number of them and, from what they have told me, Democratic deception is the main reason they split. One black guy with whom I spoke on the matter told me the following about Democrats and why he left his old party:

> *I've been Democrat since the JFK-MLK days, and it took me all this time to realize just how corrupt my own party was. Instead of telling the truth, all they do is lie, for their own gain, and try to claim accomplishments that are not even theirs. Republicans won the Civil War, freed the slaves, passed the Civil Rights Act in 1960, desegregated the schools, got Welfare reform passed and gave women their right to vote. These accomplishments are what shaped our society in so many ways, so how can it be a bad thing to be a Republican? When people say the Pledge of Allegiance, they say, "…and to the Republic for which it stands"—not "…and to the Democrats!" You know what I mean? And I don't have time for all of that ridiculousness. Obama is weak, Hillary is really crooked, and Trump is strong. And I know I can trust him. That's just the way it is, man.*

I was *so* inspired after talking to this man! He truly gets it! And everything he said is true about all of those Republican accomplishments that so many Democrats have been misinformed about for all of these years. The Democrats did not win the Civil War, and they murdered Abraham Lincoln, a Republican, for freeing the slaves. Knowing this, why would an African American even *want* to join the same party that wanted to keep Negroes enslaved? I even remember reading a report revealing that the first Grand Wizard of the KKK was honored at the 1868 Democratic National Convention. There is so much information out there that black Democrats do not even know, and their own party is keeping most of it from them. I have seen African American history professors who vote Democrat praise Jesse Owens and Jackie Robinson, the late famous black athletes, but even these men were Republicans. And Democrats did not even vote for the 14th Amendment, which shows just how serious they were about not wanting to grant citizenship to slaves. And Hillary Clinton vetoed Welfare reform twice, I believe. The *Republicans* had to get the bill signed. Black Democrats are starting to wake up and realize the truth, and all it takes is a certain number of them to vote Republican in order for Trump to clench the presidency, according to various reports. And many of these awakened black Democrats will prosper during the Political Renaissance, simply because they opened their minds to the truth and made the right decisions.

With all of that said, the point is that, after Trump, the standard American blueprint for political power will *never* be the same. In the same way that the rise of Mixed Martial Arts and the UFC is generally stepping up America's fighting game, the Trump movement is advancing the minds of *millions* of Americans. People know the truth now, and this truth is revising the political dynamic.

Last of all, I have been hearing some people, mostly Democrat, talk about the possibility of Donald Trump losing the election, as if that would somehow prove that he failed, which is so far from the truth, when you really think about it. As I have mentioned before, outside of politics, the Trumps and the Clintons are *friends*, and I seriously doubt that their friendship would end if Hillary wins the election, because Trump has proven himself so much on the campaign trail that he, on top of the friendship, would be an *asset* to the Clinton administration, which makes him politically useable. Plus, he is a billionaire. So, he could still get some things done on the Republican front under a Clinton administration. If

Hillary wins, that will not change the fact that Trump has inspired a new wave of political thinkers who will undoubtedly infiltrate the political establishment and lay the foundation for a Republican win in the next election. After four years of Hillary in office, believe me, at least half of the Democrats who will have voted for her during this election will be *dying* to vote her out during the next one. History with Trump has already been made, and that is something that can never be taken away. Plus, because one term of Hillary would have Democrats running for the hills, the likelihood of Trump winning the next election is a *very* real possibility. By then, he will have had enough "I told you so" evidence documented on public record that it would make the presidency a *steal*.

I personally believe that everyone who is undecided about whom to vote for should read Michael Moore's *Huffington Post* article, "5 Reasons Why Trump Will Win." When it comes to writing, this guy reminds me so much of myself, and his article is *so* on point. It is funny as hell but true to the bone. For the most part, from what I have read, the only political difference between Moore and me is that he does not support Trump, but I do. In spite of that, he has enough insight to see that a Trump win is more plausible than the political extrapolations about a Hillary victory. It seems as if Moore's projection is based on an understanding of human psychology rather than flip-flopping polls about Trump and Hillary that hold no merit. Here are some of the many facts that I agree with in his article:

> *Let's face it: Our biggest problem here isn't Trump—it's Hillary. She is hugely unpopular—nearly 70% of all voters think she is untrustworthy and dishonest. She represents the old way of politics, not really believing in anything other than what can get you elected. That's why she fights against gays getting married one moment, and the next she's officiating a gay marriage. Young women are among her biggest detractors…But the kids don't like her, and not a day goes by that a millennial doesn't tell me they aren't voting for her. No Democrat, and certainly no independent, is waking up on November 8ᵗʰ excited to run out and vote for Hillary the way they did the day Obama became president or when Bernie was on the primary ballot. The enthusiasm just isn't there. And because this election is going*

to come down to just one thing—who drags the most people out of the house and gets them to the polls—Trump right now is in the catbird seat.

Trump is just one of those people who, if he wins he wins, but if he loses he *still* wins. Some people just have that excellence about them, and Trump has never been the quitting type, anyway. He will fight until he wins, so, whether it is this election or the next one, or maybe even the one after that, eventually, the title "President Trump" will definitely be a reality. One day, you are going to wake up and see this on your television screen. And, when you do, you will subsequently realize that much of what critics and Democrats have told you about him was no more than disingenuous lies.

9

You Can Be a Political Mastermind Too: The Formula—Step-by-Step

I f you are one of those people who believe that fame, success and wealth are "blessings" bestowed upon one by "God"—or that these things are only acquired by those with "connections," inherited wealth, advanced college degrees, natural born talent or an above-average IQ—with all due respect, you are sadly mistaken. When it all boils down to it, success is a *choice* based on undeniable, doubtless, *powerful* belief. The only people who are not successful, or on the road to success, are those who have *not* chosen to wholeheartedly believe that they can *become* successful, and this lack of belief prevents them from taking the necessary actions that would *make* them successful. The primary factors that prevent them from believing are societal, religious and political brainwashing.

Most of the world's people do not think and dream BIG. This is an irrefutable fact. Here in America, we hear a lot of disdainful talk about the "One Percent," the wealthiest and most powerful among us, but the reality is that these peoples' wealth, power and influence are the result of hard work, huge thinking and extreme confidence in their abilities. And quite a number of them came from modest beginnings. Even those who are born into money have to think big, work hard and have similar confidence in order to maintain and increase their inherited wealth, and efficiently run their empires. However, whenever the One Percent becomes a topic of discussion, small thinkers seem to go out of their way to convince us that One Percenters are inherently evil, and that entering this class is virtually, if not outright, impossible. We find haters everywhere we go. But, let me tell you something: No matter how BIG your dream is, or how unconventional you are, if your willpower is intense enough, whenever you get *serious* about what you want and make a *decision* to succeed, as long as you *commit* to that decision and take the necessary actions that will set the stage for achievement, your success will come.

If you want to be successful in business, you can do it! If fame is what you want, you can have it! If you are tired of being broke or barely "keeping your head above water," you can *definitely* acquire millions, even billions. And, if a successful political career is what you want, even if you know nothing at all about "politics," you can achieve this dream as well. It does not matter if you are a high school or college dropout. You do not have to have any "connections." Once you begin to understand human psychology, you will realize that life itself is politics, and politics cannot exist without power. A "political mastermind" is *not* a politician. Rather, he or she is a charismatic master of human psychology with a Machiavellian mindset. Politicians, in the conventional sense, are relegated to the state. Political masterminds, however, can prosper *anywhere.* By understanding these terms and this reality, especially if you are a politician, you can create a platform for success in any field in which you choose to become successful. Why see yourself as a "statesman" when you can become a "worldsman"? If the human psyche is the tome upon which power itself is grounded, then, why master anything else first? Donald Trump mastered human psychology long before running for president. He knows how the human brain works and understands human politics at its deepest levels, and this is what makes it so easy for him to excel at politics of the state. He became successful by executing political mastermind strategies in business, and you can do the same thing by applying the same in whatever field you want to get into. The only thing that you are missing is a practical formula that can help you make it happen, and this chapter is about to give it to you, step-by-step. But, first, let me clarify a few things in order to assure that we are on the same page.

There is no one "formula" for success, but the "ingredients" are all the same. There are countless books on the market about success and how to attain it, but only a few are written from the mastermind perspective, especially those with political themes. If you have read this book through and through, or intend to do so at your convenience, and power and success are what you *really* want, then, the information in this chapter will definitely put you on your way to achieving the life that you want for yourself. The power game is reserved for masterminds only, and no one is *born* a mastermind. The "Mastermind Mindset," which I refer to as the "Double M," can be *learned*, and the politics of life can take you further than the politics of state ever could. Therefore, from here on out, consider this book, particularly this chapter, your *practical blueprint for power*. For a moment, rid from your mind notions of religious piety, social networking, collegiate pursuit, inborn talent and what "they" say about the human IQ. Focus on *reality*, and the reality is this: Last year, according to *The Daily Caller*, a record 920,000 people became millionaires, with more than a third of them residing here in the United Sates. If they can enter the millionaire bracket, just imagine what *you* can do.

Before getting to the formula, I would also like to discuss "haters" for a second. If you want to succeed and become the best that you can ever be, then, you need to accept the fact that, on the road to success, you will encounter people, even some who you really care about, who will, for more reasons than I can count, try to stop you from making it BIG. The bigger your dream, the more haters you will have, and there is no way around it. Church members, family members, friends, spouses, colleagues and even strangers will try to instill doubt in you. People around you who think small will *never* comprehend a dream as BIG as yours. If you can take this in stride and keep pushing toward your goals, then, you already have what it takes to succeed. However, if you are not secure in yourself, in the end, you will end up going to your grave with a lot of unrealized dreams and potential, all because someone told you that you could not do something—and you believed it. Powerful people do not care what others think of them and, if you fall into this category, then, you are only a few millimeters away from your success. Now, "the formula."

How to Become a "Political Mastermind"

A couple pages back, I mentioned that a political mastermind is not a politician, but rather "a charismatic master of human psychology with a Machiavellian mindset," and I meant every word of it. Due to the status quo, conventional minds define "politics" in a governmental way that is contrary to reality; therefore, in order to take full advantage of the success formula that follows, we have to modify our perception of politics. While contemporary definitions describe politics as "activities that relate to influencing the actions and policies of a government or getting and keeping power in a government," in order to understand the true meaning of politics, we have to look at the etymology of this word. I recently found an article on Wikipedia that best explains it. Here is what it says:

> **Politics** *(from Greek: πολιτικός politikos, definition "of, for, or relating to citizens") is the process of making uniform decisions applying to all members of a group. It also involves the use of power by one person to affect the behavior of another person. More narrowly, it refers to achieving and exercising positions of governance—organized control over a human community, particularly a state... It is very often said that politics is about power...History of political thought can be traced back to early antiquity, with seminal works such as Plato's Republic, Aristotle's Politics and the works of Confucius...Many people view formal politics as something outside of themselves...Informal Politics is understood as forming alliances, exercising power and protecting and advancing particular ideas or goals. Generally, this includes anything affecting one's daily life, such as the way an office or household is managed, or how one person or group exercises influence over another. Informal Politics is typically understood as everyday politics, hence the idea that "politics is everywhere."*

As you can see, the true nature of politics has nothing to do with government—it is simply a way of life concerning power. Utilization of strategy, based on an understanding of human psychology, with the intent to influence the behavior of others in order to *acquire* power, is what politics is, by original definition. Formality is the offspring of conventionalism, but informality is the epitome of reality. Thus, in order to succeed in life, business or government on any major scale, one has to master human psychology and strategically use this mastery to influence the behavior of others in a way that makes success attainable. Adopting this realistic perspective makes the pursuit of power all the more easy, because *true* "political" awareness is the only thing that can make a success formula actually work. With that said, here is the "formula," in depth.

"Political Mastermind" Success Formula—Step-by-Step

Anyone who wants to become a political mastermind (i.e., enter a state of mind that enables one to acquire power and have whatever it is that he or she wants, no matter how BIG) has to follow a series of practical "steps" that will, if applied rightly, take his or her mind to the next level. For your convenience, I have devised nine primary steps, to be exact, with each of them sufficiently explicated. Simple enough for virtually anyone to understand, they are as follows. If you are absolutely serious about acquiring power and success, please, pay attention:

STEP 1

Know what you **want**, *not what you* **need**, *and make a decision to go after it, with* **no** *exceptions.*

When you know what you want, this places you in a more powerful position that is conducive to power and success, because most of the people around you have absolutely no idea what they want. Why? Because they are too focused on what they are *lacking*, on what they *need*. Even though conventional thought tells us to "focus on what we need, rather than what we want," in reality, it would be stupid to focus more on needs than wants. *What we need is what we do not have*, and, if we consistently focus on what we do not have, which is a negative vibration, we will only perpetuate the state of not having. The Universe responds to and gives us whatever we think about most, so, if we focus more on what we want, which is a positive vibration, what we want will come, and lack, consequently, will be eliminated. Additionally, we all have needs but, if we do not *want* what we need badly enough, we will never get it. For example, in our society, most of the most common needs are money for bills, food and shelter; decent-paying employment; efficient transportation; and, as some would argue, companionship. However, even though many of us say and know that we need these things, we focus so much on not having them that we end up not seriously wanting them enough to get them. Consequently, we end up with a ton of bills that we cannot pay, our refrigerators virtually empty, no residence to call our own, depending on others for transportation and our love lives in all kinds of unhappy states—all because we are too focused on the present, the need, the lack, the "bad" or "fucked up" end of the stick. We keep telling the same story and believing it, which keeps us stuck in a seemingly perpetual rut. We keep attracting what we think about most. However, if we bring ourselves to focus on the opposite of lack and actually see ourselves having it, loving it and enjoying it, our story, as well as our situation, will change. And this is why it is so important to focus more on what we want than what we need.

In addition, there is no point in knowing what you want if you have not made a decision to go after it. A lot of people say that they want something but, when you look at their actions, it becomes obvious that they are not *serious* about what they want, and it becomes virtually impossible for you to even take them seriously at all. They may make a few strides toward their goal here and there, but they spend so much time either doing nothing, or bouncing around from project to project, that they never really complete anything. They spend so much time procrastinating and complaining about small stuff that completion becomes all the more fleeting, and they blame everything and everyone that they can think of for the lack that they have created themselves. These kinds of people are so anti-successful that, although they may have some good qualities that make you like them, in the end, it is not even worth your time being around them. Their penchant for negative thought can mess up your positive vibe in an instant and hinder your success. If you know someone like this, then, he or she is a personal example of what you should *not* be or become, under any circumstances. And you know yourself better than anybody does. Therefore, if this paragraph and the one above describe you, and you know it, this means that you have to make some changes in your life that will make you more worthy of success. If you know what you want, make a decision to go after it with all of your might, and commit to that decision with all of your being, with no exceptions. Only you hold the power to make that decision, because no one outside of yourself is in control of your life—only you are. By knowing what you want, going after it with commitment and giving virtually no thought at all to what you lack, you will put yourself in a position to attain power and accomplish success.

STEP 2

Refuse to think small, because power and success can only be acquired by thinking BIG!

Everything around us has been created by people who, at some point in time, refused to think trivially. However, in spite of this, it seems as if people are still hell-bent on thinking *small*. The leaders that we elect, the technology that we use, and the creators of all of the products that we buy are all linked to beyond-average thinking. When Donald Trump decided to run for president, countless critics ridiculed him in an attempt to persuade the public that he, a multibillionaire businessman with no "political" experience at all, would *never* win in the Republican primaries or clench the Republican presidential nomination. For example, last year, in 2015, I read an article in *The Atlantic* by James Fallows that has now been proven untrue. In this article, entitled "3 Truths About Trump: The Passions Evoked by Donald Trump Deserve Notice—His 'Candidacy' Does not," Fallows asserts that Trump "will not be the 45th president of the United States." He also says, "The chance of his winning nomination and election is exactly zero." Several months later, however, Trump won the Republican nomination for president by a *landslide*. When Steve Jobs told people that he would create Apple, Inc., some did not believe him, either. However, he thought BIG and turned his product into an international phenomenon. And, when Royce Gracie talked about making his UFC dream a reality, people doubted him, too. But he stuck to his vision and, now, the Ultimate Fighting Championship is one of America's most favorite pastimes.

See, people who think BIG do not waste time focusing on where they are—they focus on where they *want* to be. When they encounter small thinkers, they say to themselves, "Fuck what *other* people think. I'm doing *me!*" When certain people found out that I was writing a book on Donald Trump from the strategy-based, mastermind perspective, they tried every trick in the book to stop me from writing it, including many of those from my own ethnic community, who seemed to have some kind of personal vendetta against whites that causes them to take their frustrations out on Trump, his movement and his supporters. "Donald Trump is a racist," so many of them told me. "You're only wasting your time writing a book about him." But their use of the race card only inspired me more because, on top of the fact that I have never seen or heard The Donald fabricating reality as it regards African Americans, thinking outside of the box and going against the color grain is kind of my own personal slap in the face to conventionalism.

When I first read about how inventor Thomas Edison failed 1,000 times before creating the light bulb, and how his childhood teachers always told his parents that he would never be successful because of his "slow brain," I began to understand the power of thinking BIG, because it was obvious that, if someone with a "slow" brain could dream BIG and die rich, then, someone with a "fast brain" who thinks small would most likely die poor. Additionally, Larry Ellison, co-founder of a database management company called Software Development Laboratories, grew up poor, has never met his birth father, and did not find out that he was adopted until later in life. Now, according to *Business Insider*, he has an estimated net worth of $46.2 billion. He has planes, yachts, several mansions, and even an entire Hawaiian island. Obviously, he has not gotten where he is today by thinking small. And there are millions of other success stories out there about the abundance acquired by those who absolutely refused to think small. Even *evil* people who have enough sense to think bigger than average end up becoming powerful and successful, which proves that moral notions of good and bad mean nothing. The Universe, God or whatever you want to call it responds only to emitted vibrations. Thus, success does not come to those who think negatively about it and are content with thinking small and having small things—and the same is true of power. We are all who we are, and where we are today, because of the way that we have been thinking all of these years. If we do not have shit, and we are not on the road to having shit and doing BIG things, this is nobody's fault but our own. Think small, and that is exactly what you will be—small. But think BIG and, eventually, abundance will flow to you. If this applies to you, and you know that you have been thinking small and getting nowhere, either step up your game or commit suicide, because you are already walking around dead. It does not get any realer than that. Period.

STEP 3

*Do what you **love**, not what you **like**, **because passion that comes from what one loves to do emits vibrations that accelerate the Law of Attraction.***

Let us get one thing understood: As the old sayings go, in life, no matter what you are doing, you will only "get out of it whatever you put into it" and "the bigger the risk, the greater the reward." Most people claim that they "already know this" but, like I always tell people, it is not about what you know that makes you smart, powerful or successful—it is about what you *apply*. Moreover, if people are not passionate about what they do, almost always, they end up becoming slaves to the "system," especially inside of the workforce. In pursuit of their dreams, most people do only the bare minimum and, when they fail, instead of acknowledging and accepting the fact that they did not go hard enough for what they wanted, which decreased their attraction power, they find every excuse in the book to justify why they failed. We see examples of this daily in business, politics and virtually everywhere else. And, at the end of the day, their failure boils down to only one thing: they spent too much time wasting time on what they like or do not like, rather than what they *love*.

Everything that we do emits vibrations. But our thoughts and feelings yield the strongest vibrational discharge of all. Because the Universe responds to how we think and feel, the results of our thoughts and feelings are twofold: If we think small and do not feel abundant before abundance comes, our attraction power gets weaker and weaker, which drastically decreases our chances of accomplishing our goals. We emit low vibrations, so the Universe gives us low manifestation. But, when we feel confident about what we want, knowing that it will come to us eventually, our feelings change, and no one can tell us that we are not already abundant, because we can see and feel whatever it is that we want before we even receive it. The vibrations we emit, therefore, are positive, strong and *accelerate* attraction. Everything that we want begins to come to us in countless ways, and the more positively we think and feel about it, the faster it seems to come. Nothing is elusive, and understanding this Universal truth will definitely facilitate one's attainment of power, wealth and success.

I know one particular individual who has so many excuses for failure that it is pitiful. This person has tremendous talent but spends countless hours complaining about work, life, the past and how much she hates her job and, one day, all of the incessant griping compelled me to ask her a simple but very serious question. "What is your *passion*?" I asked her. "Above all, when it comes to what you truly *love* doing, what *moves* you, exactly?" Her response to me was:

> *I like doing music, but I don't like the music business, the music industry. I like travelling, but I don't like all of the stuff that comes with it. I like making stuff, like jewelry, and I used to sell custom jewelry back in high school, but no one even buys custom jewelry anymore. But I love singing, though. Every time I sing, I feel free. But it's so hard to make it in the [music] industry today without having to sell your soul to the Devil that I'm really not even passionate about that anymore. And I work so much that I wouldn't even have the time to sing if I wanted to. But I like my job, even though I want to quit sometimes. I've put in for raises, but they never promote me. I don't think that's right, but I'm still trying to figure it all out.*

As you can see, because of the way that she thinks, this individual will probably never become successful, much less powerful. I asked her about her passion and what she *loved*, and she responded by telling me about what she *liked*. On top of that, her constant use of the word "but" indicates that her confidence level is extremely low, and she is cynical beyond description, which only brings a bundle of negative attraction her way.

Now, contrast that with the following. I recently discussed all of this with a young friend of mine, who is 22 years old, but from a slightly different perspective, to point out to him the important of passion where the pursuit of power, success and wealth are concerned. I asked him, "Have you ever been in love? And, if so, when you're in love, when you're either with or away from your sweetheart, how does love make you feel?" And this is what he told me:

When I'm in love, it's like everything I do revolves around that person. No matter what I'm doing, she's a part of it. If I'm hanging out with friends, most of the time, she's coming with me. And, when we're not together, we're always talking on the phone. It's like I can't stop thinking about her, and it makes me feel good.

The main reason I posed the above question was to point out to my friend that, if one could be as passionate about one's dreams as one is about a significant other when in love, one would never know what it is like to *not* succeed, because that passionate vibration would set the Law of Attraction aflame, all to one's benefit. But most people just do not get it.

Think about your career and ask yourself, "Am I doing something that I *like*, something that I *do not* like, or something that I absolutely *love*?" What is your *passion*? If your job is not your passion, then, you should not be doing it, especially if you do not even like it—unless you are using it as a stepping stone to get where you want to be. If you are not already plotting your escape from the workforce so that you can do your own thing, then, the workforce is simply a waste of your time, because it will never make you as rich and successful as your passion and dream can. If you allow yourself to become a wage or salary slave, and never make your passion your primary focus, eventually, you will just end up like the majority of people who keep their jobs "because they have to." All you will be able to think about is bills, bills, bills. Believe me, if you start thinking success, success, success, no job, no matter *how* good the pay, would ever truly hold your attention for long, because it would never truly excite you when you awaken in the morning. If, sometimes, you do not even want to go to work at all, wishing that you could have the day off to rest or spend time doing something else—especially something that you *love* to do—then, you know that an employee is *not* what you want to be for the rest of your life.

The most powerful people in the world are not employees, they are owners. And the wealthiest and most successful do not spend their time doing things that they do not like—they spend the bulk of their time doing what they *love*. If ever you bring yourself to do the same, eventually, you will never have to go around knocking on success' door—it will proudly come banging on yours. Believe it!

STEP 4

Be different, *never conventional, and follow your instincts at all cost, because your purpose-driven spirit never lies.*

Have you ever wondered why some people become famous, rich, successful and powerful, but most others do not? If so, have you ever come up with an answer that explains this? If not, let me sum it for you, in brief: The people who make it BIG in life make it big because, aside from the fact that they *think* BIG, they are DIFFERENT. What I mean by this is that they *defy* convention. They go against the grain and create their *own* road to success, knowing that the conventional way of doing things is completely out of tune with reality. When pursuing their dreams, they learn only what they *need* to learn, take the best from it and discard the rest. Their instincts let them know exactly what they have to do, and they do it the best way they can. Their *minds* are different. Their *styles* are different. So are their behaviors, attitudes and outlooks on life. Basically, while everyone else is following trends and adopting ideologies, they are creating their own—just by being themselves. And the Universe rewards them abundantly. This could be you!

In this world, it takes *courage* to think outside of the box. Most of the people around you are so trapped inside the Social Matrix that they think it is "crazy" for someone to question reality and "established truths." All they know is what they have been taught, and this is the worst thing that can happen to a person, because this kind of mindset tends to keep the human brain enslaved forever. Until one can bring oneself to think in terms of reality, one can never be mentally free.

The spirit inside of you is *purpose*-driven. What this means is that you were put here on earth for a purpose that is uniquely yours—no one else's. What one calls your "instinct" is really your inner spirit speaking to you and, when you listen to it, trust and believe, it will *never* lead you wrong. If the world around you is moving in one direction, but "something inside of you" is passionately telling you to move in another, then, that is exactly what you should do. Powerful people do not follow crowds—the crowds follow *them*. And, though you may not believe or understand what I am about to tell you, in time, you will:

The Essence of you was not put here by anything or anyone other than Itself. Before it came here, it chose to come— you chose to come—and It/You did not come here to follow convention. Both came to make convention follow them.

Your purpose here on earth, as is everyone else's, is to do BIG things in your *own* BIG way. Most people, however, just get so caught up in this fleshly, mundane world of sensation that they forget about their purpose. They are inside of a body, believing that they *are* the body, and this only suppresses their Spirit. Instead of Universally Spiritual, they become irreversibly physical, their purpose never fully realized. Without purpose, there is no guidance. With no guidance, these people get lost. This is why the blind is always following the blind, and the blind will never have your best interest—only that "thing," that "Spirit," that *desire* inside of you does. It never lies, and you know this from the way that it moves and energizes you *internally* in a way that you can *feel*.

Every person who has ever risen to power underwent the same experience. Therefore, if power and success are what you want, you have to dare to be different and heed your purpose in the game of human politics. Take pride in being atypical and uncommon. Embrace the "out of the ordinary." Who gives a damn if "they" think that you are "strange," "odd," "bizarre," "peculiar" or "weird?" The Universe is one of the strangest things that most people will never understand, but they are fascinated by it still. And the Universe is where you came from. You are a part of it, which means that it is natural for you to be misunderstood. When Karl Friedrich Benz was masterminding his plan to create the world's first true automobile, most of the people around him thought he was weird too—until he proved them wrong and rode right past them, as if they had never even existed. They had been riding and using animals for so long that they could not think beyond an animalistic level, and not much has changed since then, which is why it is essential for you to champion your own status over that of the status quo. As the late, social critic Desiderius Erasmus Roterodamus stated way back in the 16th century, "In the land of the blind, the one-eyed man is king." The world is waiting on YOU, so never let social custom dumb you down. Be *different*, go with your *gut* and shock the *entire* world! Check the historical record: this is how power is acquired and legends are made.

STEP 5

Always *go hard, because focus is the primary discipline of a master, and those who "go soft" inevitably become losers.*

For as long as I can remember, I have always had the ability to focus, and focus *hard*. I have never been the kind of person to start on something that gets pushed aside and neglected for long, because I understand the power of completion. When I get into something, I go harder than hard—I go berserk. And, by doing so, I have been able to accomplish things that countless people assumed was "impossible." And the most interesting thing of all is that I accomplished most of it by going against the grain. I did it in my own way, created my own style, on my own time and broke virtually all the rules. I was so hungry for whatever I was pursuing that I went over and beyond to finish whatever I started, with the intention of doing it better than everyone around me, but in a unique way that no one had ever done before. I excelled at it, and most of it was self-taught. English, writing, Spanish, American Sign Language, college, public speaking, Krav Maga—whatever I got into to, I went hard and mastered it. Oftentimes, most of the people around me who shared the same interest were astonished by my acquired skills, convinced that I was simply a "natural" at it all. What normally took them years to master, I mastered in months. And, over time, after watching their study habits, I became convinced that my proficiency had nothing to do with prodigy—I just went harder than they did. They were too hell-bent on "going soft" and eventually became losers in life. I am 33 now but still have the same mindset and ability, just more advanced. I have experienced some of the harshest things a human being can ever experience in life, but came back stronger every time. Not because I am "special." Not because I am "chosen." And, definitely, not because I am "privileged," because such has never been my reality. It is because I go hard, and I cannot reiterate this enough. When you aim for a goal, the Universe respects nothing else. If you are the go-hard type, then, you know exactly what I mean. If not, then, it is time for you to step up your game, because I do not know, and have never heard of, any mastermind on the face of the planet who is too soft and unfocused to go hard. When you want something badly, hard is the only way to go, and anyone who denies this should be eye-gouged by his or her own ignorance.

People who get rich, and stay rich, never go soft. They never "sleep"—until they make it. And, even then, they still manage to go hard. Instead of being dead while awake, they prefer to sleep when they die, because there is simply too much to do and accomplish. They understand that death is the equivalent of life of total lack of life-motivated motion, and this is what keeps them focused. Whenever you are fired up by a BIG idea, in that moment, it is time for you to act, with no excuses. Every second that you waste through procrastination only pushes your goal further and further away. The time is NOW, and the "Vortex of Opportunity" is wide open, just waiting on you. If your willpower is not strong enough, and you do not correct that, you will never succeed. Negative energy will kill your drive, the crabs in the barrel will pull you down, you will lose focus and devote your time and attention to everything but the right thing. Obstacles will hinder you, and all of this will culminate in the abortion of the baby that is called your "passion." Is this what you really want, or do you want to be a winner? Do you want people to continue not taking you seriously, or do you want honest recognition? Do you want power, wealth, influence and authority, or do you want to go to your deathbed knowing that, after all of these years on earth, the only thing that you have amounted to is being a nobody? These are some very serious questions. No one respects anyone with a penchant for "going soft," as Bob Dole's wife would probably attest (pun intended).

But let me tell you about losers. There are two kinds: (1) Those who never amount to anything in life, and (2) those who follow their dreams, accomplish them, and, then, fall off, without the guts and willpower to get back up and go hard again. I know people in both categories and, to hammer this point a little more, let me give you a couple examples.

The Faker Who Will Never Make It

My wife, Sheron, has met some pretty cool celebrities in her lifetime, mostly during her younger years, when she was pursuing her dream of becoming an actress and Hip-Hop/R&B recording artist in the late 1990s. Denzel Washington, Mary J. Blige, Wyclef Jean, Angie Stone, Sean Lennon, Pink, Fred Davis (son of Clive Davis), Hillary Beckford (Tyson Beckford's mom), Grammy-nominated music producer Deric

"D-Dot" Angelettie—and many, many others—have crossed her path. Because of this, as well as her former, unofficial title as the "Networking Queen of Manhattan," her social circle expanded by leaps and bounds. She has a lot of friends, most of whom are pretty good people, and people just seem to gravitate to her, as they do me. However, as you probably already know in regard to friendship, not *all* "friends" stick around for a lifetime. There is always that *one* sour apple that is hell-bent on sabotaging companionship over something petty and, recently, Sheron and I personally experienced this.

Before marrying me, my wife had one particular "friend" who seemed to be destined for stardom. Let us call her "Katrina." Her father was rich, and all she ever talked about was success and wealth. She had a business coach, frequently attended wealth-based seminars and events, established an independent company, and even ghostwrote several books. By all appearances, she really had it going on. It seemed that Sheron and she were boon companions. A few months later, their friendship morphed into a business relationship, in which Katrina agreed to provide a certain service to Sheron for a respectable fee. An initial payment was made, the service was initiated, but later went south for various reasons, which was not a big deal, and they just continued on with their friendship. Everything seemed to be going great—until I stepped into the picture.

The first time I met Katrina, I thought she was cool. However, my instinct subsequently told me that something about her was just not right, and it did not take long for me to discover that my intuition was correct. Out of the blue, she just started acting shady with me, all because my work schedule hindered me from picking up an appliance that she offered as a gift to Sheron and me. Instead of understanding this and allowing us to reschedule the pickup, she began harboring animosity toward me. Not long after, it seemed as if her animosity had turned into full-blown hate, and this began to affect my marriage. When Sheron and I were facing challenges in our wedlock, she did everything in her power to try to turn my wife against me, to no avail. Not only did she deny Sheron a safe haven for head space when we were going through it, but also she talked extremely negatively about *both* of us, with emphasis on me, of course, and I wondered what would make a woman so profoundly bitter towards men. Eventually, I got my answer.

After doing a little digging, I discovered that Perfect Little Ms. Patty was not so perfect after all and, with what I know, it is a shame that she even tried to appear as such. I had already known that she was an undercover lesbian, but that was not a problem, because I not only *love* lesbians but also hold the LGBTQ community in high regard, due to its fearlessness in the face of pure ignorance, bias, prejudice, racism and flat out violence and hate, especially its fight for justice and equality. It was all of the other stuff I found out about her that shattered the illusion she presented to the world.

Katrina had a reputation for seducing and using women to get what she wanted, and the people I talked to described her as a "leech." For various reasons, her literary works did not move the units that she said she wanted, and she started failing miserably at her business endeavors, which eventually led to her getting evicted from her apartment for defaulting on her rent. And I firmly believe that the aforementioned appliance gift was offered by her with an ulterior motive, which explains why she flipped out when I could not pick it up. After all of this, she was essentially homeless, bouncing around from pillow to post, and even asked my wife if she could come reside with us for a week, to which we humbly declined. I also heard her referred to as an "extreme, man-hating feminist," and that description *surely* seemed to fit, due to her behavior toward me, and her many comments to others about men in general. She also seemed to be exceedingly, religiously confused. I was told that she was once a Christian who became a member of the Black Hebrew Israelites faith (where she once fell into a ditch, while considered unclean, and all the male members refused to touch her), and that she now follows The Mother Goddess belief system and conducts a series of "rituals" for a variety of reasons. She was also a proficient weed head with a penchant for smoking up everyone else's marijuana. It seemed as if she was always penniless and, from the information I gathered, she was ousted from her own family, for god-knows-what. After discovering all of this, I was completely blown away. Last I heard, she was seducing some elderly woman in order to have a place to stay, and defaulted on her rent with this lady too (shaking my head)!

Anyway, all of the above, in my opinion, is what makes Katrina a loser. From what I gather, she has never truly gone hard for *anything* in life, tried to "fake it until she made it," and ended up failing miserably in both life *and* business. Many wealthy people would probably argue that the likelihood of her ever becoming powerful and successful is zero to none and, based on what I know about human psychology, I would surely concur with this assertion. As for her ever becoming a political mastermind, that is a no-brainer. I do not think that she has what it takes to truly go hard because, if all of the information I acquired is true, and I believe it is, she is too miserable to do anything but go soft. If ever you encounter someone like this, take my word for it: expel this person from your world as soon as possible. Misery loves company, so let these kinds of people keep company with themselves. Enough said.

Those Who Make It, but Fall Off and Give Up

Most people who say that they go hard usually do not go hard enough. With whatever they are doing, they start out with a burst of energy that results in some kind of short-lived accomplishment but, after that, they eventually slow down. Before you know it, for them, going hard becomes an afterthought—because all they ever end up doing is going soft. We see examples of this virtually *everywhere* we go: with new employees in the workforce, countless athletes in sports, newcomers in entertainment, budding entrepreneurs in business and numerous politicians in government. They come in so *hard*, so *focused*, that they eclipse everyone around them. In addition, the mass media, as sensationalized as it is, tends to ride these kinds of waves, always depicting these newbies as "hot" or "the next big thing." And, then, most of these people fall off and do not even seem relevant anymore. Some of them go hard and bounce back bigger and better than ever, but most never return to their former greatness. This is why, for those of you who seek power, it is extremely important for you to go hard and never lose focus. The moment that you lose sight of your goal, you are finished. This is just the way it is.

I met a rich guy like this a couple days ago who seemed to fit this description. You may or may not know who he is, but you have probably seen or heard some of his work. His birth name is Jamal Fincher Jones but, professionally, he goes by the name Polow Da Don. He is an American super producer, songwriter and rapper who has worked with some of the biggest names in the entertainment industry, including but not limited to Rihanna, Usher, Will Smith, Christina Aguilera, Nelly, Nicki Minaj, Fergie, Limp Bizkit, Keri Hilson, T.I., Chris Brown, Kelis and Ciara. The Grammy Award-winning singer, Monica, is his cousin, and his net worth sits somewhere around $25 and $42 million. The weirdest thing, though, is that, prior to meeting him, I had never even heard of him before. He needed some help moving from one residence to another, and this is where I came into play.

Upon entering his residence, I noticed that there were many plaques on the walls, which caught my attention. Upon inspection, I discovered that most of these plaques were for his BMI accomplishments, and I remember seeing a Billboard plaque from February 10, 2007—an accomplishment for the "Promise" record that he produced for Ciara, which hit #1 on the Billboard charts. He was asleep when I, and a few of my colleagues, entered his dwelling, escorted by a woman who I believe was a substitute assistant. However, later, he awakened and, by that time, my partners and I were fully aware of who he was. When he finally started moving about, we noticed that something was off. Not only was he impolite and discourteous, refusing to speak to the very people he had hired to help him move, but also he was distant and seemed very depressed. At some point, he left, and later called said "assistant," inquiring about how long the job would last. During one of these calls, he allegedly tried to get her to go outside of her job title to help pack and move boxes in order to expedite the moving process, which really pissed her off. And I found out about this because one of my partners and I overheard her talking negatively about Don to someone else via cell phone. Here is what we overheard her saying, in paraphrase:

> *I ain't his assistant! I don't pack and move boxes! It ain't the same no more, and he's just depressed because he ain't been hot since "Throw Some D's On It."*

What she was referring to was the once hot rap song by Rich Boy entitled "Throw Some D's," featuring Polow Da Don, and she was pissed. Her statement seemed to confirm our suspicions: Polow was just one of those guys who once pursued his dreams, went hard as hell to accomplish them, then attained them—but eventually got too "comfortable," stopped going hard and ended up in a state of depression. Basically, the type who, in spite of having money in the bank, went from being a winner to a loser. We were at his crib for about five hours, were scheduled to return the following day, and he did not provide a tip at all. I had some other work to do the next day, and needed more time to focus on this manuscript, so I did not return for the second portion of the job. I was just told, a few minutes ago, that the second day at his residence was not much different than the first, and that the multimillionaire producer did not tip that day as well. I ended up making less money on the other job, but felt a whole lot better, because I was not in an environment in which misery seemed to love company.

Truth be told, I feel somewhat sorry for Polow, because I hate seeing people feeling down and depressed. There is so much more that he could be doing with his time and energy. Put "Polow Da Down has gotten fat" into almost any major Internet search engine and you will see exactly what I mean. A lot of people say that they want success, but when they get it, they stop going hard. And most people never even go hard enough to get it at all. Masterminds, on the other hand, do not have it in them to go soft. At the end of the day, it all boils downs to how badly you want whatever it is that you claim you want—and how serious you are about keeping and increasing it once you get it. I believe that the likelihood of Polow Da Don making a major comeback is incredibly slim. Unless he reads this book, gets pissed off about me telling the truth and channels that frustration into something positive, like motivation, I cannot envision him doing anything else but going soft.

It seems as if I am always rubbing shoulders with TV stars and celebrities who, by all appearances, seem cool on the surface, but turn out to be losers. This experience with Polow Da Don reminds me of another experience I had with reality TV star Mimi Faust from VH1's hit show *Love & Hip Hop: Atlanta*, when I helped her move into her new home a few months ago. A few of my colleagues and I were there for three days. We stayed approximately 10 hours on the first day, 9 or 10 hours the second day, and about 7 hours on the third.

Prior to this job, as with Polow, I did not even know who she was, per se. It was not until a briefing that I remembered hearing about a "Mimi" a year or two earlier during a sex tape scandal I had once read about in a magazine and, at that time, I was never really into Reality TV shows at all. However, one of my colleagues was a fan of the show and updated me about her, with emphasis on the sex tape, and that is when I remembered who she was: Nikko London's ex-girlfriend. I told my wife about it, and we watched a few *Love & Hip Hop: Atlanta* episodes, to see what all the hype was about. We both agreed that it was a pretty cool show, and that Mimi seemed really cool, sweet, classy and somewhat innocent. So, that was my perception of her. The next day, my colleagues and I loaded up and headed out to her residence.

From the moment we entered her home, we had to deal primarily with her assistant, who was cool, cute and funny, with a very bubbly personality. A few minutes later, she summoned Mimi, who was upstairs in her room. When she came downstairs, the first thing that shocked us about her was the fact that, in person, she looked *nothing* like she did on television. There was no makeup, no cameras—just her in her natural state. She was wearing baggy clothes, her hair was kind of messy, and it seemed as if she had just gotten out of bed. She did not look like a TV star at all. By all appearances, she looked like a regular person. And her ass looked *flat*. In my opinion, she was cute, but not very attractive. Of course, none of that mattered, because I was there to take care of business. That is it.

To make a long story short, during our time there, Mimi eventually warmed up to us all. The funniest thing I remember her asking me, after looking down at my feet, was, "Dang, what size shoe do you wear?" after playfully joking about how huge my feet are. I playfully responded, "A size 14, big and wide," and we laughed. She even ate chicken with us during one of our breaks—Popeye's, I believe, which, for the record, she did not purchase. And, initially, she actually looked out of place eating it, while we all chatted about where we were from, as if she were overly concerned about her weight and staying thin. In spite of this, however, she eventually devoured that chicken like the rest of us. I also remember her mentioning to us that she did not know much about cooking. The time we all spent together during that meal kind of felt like a bonding experience.

But that was just one element of the experience, the one that sort of reinforced my aforementioned perception of her, based on what I saw on television. However, there were two additional elements: one that made me feel sorry for her, and another that showed me how much of a *loser* she is. Let me tell you about those, in brief.

What made me feel sorry for her was an instance in which a few of my colleagues and I noticed a Ziploc bag with a decent amount of pills resting atop one of her nightstands. Instantly, upon noticing what we were looking at, she snatched up the bag and said, "What's this? Where did this come from? I don't know what this is!" She seemed to be feigning shock and behaving suspiciously, as if she were trying to protect some kind of secret. Then, she walked off with the pill bag—and the pills were never seen again. As for what kinds of pills they were,

I cannot say, for certain, but they definitely looked like a mixture of uppers, antidepressants, Mollies and Xanax. All I can say about it is this: If the pills were prescribed, why would they be in a Ziploc bag, instead of in their own individual bottles? And why hide the pills, anyway? When I was at Polow Da Don's crib, emptying the kitchen cabinets, there were prescribed pills in one particular cabinet, and he left the premises without taking them. Why? Because he had nothing to hide and, if I remember correctly, the pills were prescribed for health-related purposes. He did not snatch up the bottles and disappear with them, like Mimi did. As far as the pills go, though, I will just let you be the judge.

Anyway, I remember thinking to myself, "*Damn.* If that's what I think it is in that bag, that's fucked up. She must be trying to escape reality." I started paying attention to her behavior after that, wondering if she was "high" on something while we were there. Then, sometime later, her behavior convinced me that she probably was. I overheard her fussing with an Xfinity representative via cell phone, and observed her pacing back and forth while attempting to have her cable turned on. She was *hot*! Then, all of a sudden, during the call, she started bawling out crying. Given the way that she was crying, one would have thought that she had just been dumped by a spouse of 10 years. However, from my observation, it was simply because of her not being able to have her cable turned on. Upon seeing this, I wondered if her excessive display of emotion was linked to the pills. Though I could not be certain, I still felt sorry for her. "Whoever thought a 'tough' woman like her would bawl out, off camera?" I thought. She looked so pitiful, and that particular incident is what officially killed my interest in so-called Reality TV.

What really showed me how much of a loser she was, though, were two things, in particular. On one occasion, I saw her flashing numerous hundred-dollar bills in front of two of my female colleagues, in what seemed like an attempt to impress them. However, at the end of the job, as with Polow Da Don, she did not even tip her workers. Of course, we did not give a shit, but it was the principle of it all that mattered. And, on another occasion, not long before we left, she did something that completely blew my mind—the severity of which I had not discovered until later that night.

While downstairs in her old home, two of my colleagues and I were preparing boxes for packing and transport, when Mimi approached. She then pointed to several items inside of a nearby closet and began explaining to us which items she wanted transported to her new home, and which ones she did not. Then, she pointed at a particular suitcase and began talking negatively about her former boyfriend, Nikko London, and made a few additional comments about *Love & Hip Hop: Atlanta*. Regarding Nikko and the suitcase, however, here is what she said, as I recall it:

> *This is Nikko's shit [pointing at the suitcase]. I don't want it, and it's been in here long enough. Fuck Nikko. Fuck him. You can have it. I'm serious—take it all.*

Frankly, we were *shocked*! I remember us all standing there looking at one another, like, "Wow. She just went off the deep end, flipped out for nothing. She must really hate Nikko." Of course, none of us said this aloud, but I could tell that we were all thinking the same thing. We attempted to refuse the offer, but she insisted and continued speaking negatively about Nikko, in a way that made it clear that she wanted his stuff out of there, as if it were cursed. Therefore, so that we could continue doing our job, we accepted the offer, removed the suitcase from the house, agreed to check its contents later and went back to work. But I remember thinking to myself, "What kind of woman would do such a thing with a man's personal belongings?" My answer: a bitter woman.

Anway, later that night, after the job was over and we were preparing to head home, I retrieved the suitcase and lay it atop the trunk of my car, so that my colleagues and I could see what it contained. Upon opening it, a scent of freshness hit my nose, and what we all saw did not seem that important at first. By all appearances, the suitcase contained clothing only—pants, shorts, shirts, "New York Vault Safe Crackers" skull caps, other headgear and even the man's socks and boxers. Talk about *bitter*. From the unmistakable, clean, laundry-like scent, I gathered that Mimi, or someone who works for her, must have collected these items, washed them and packed it all into the suitcase. I could be wrong about that, but that is what it seemed like, given the scent. Before I could even ask my sometimes-crazy colleagues (and I mean "crazy" in a *fond* manner) what they would like to do with the items, their hands began moving so quickly, going in and out of the suitcase, that I was humorously at a loss for words. As normally done with gifts from customers, they began divvying up the items amongst themselves, and I decided to keep what was left in the suitcase until I could figure out what to do with it all. Then, I zipped up the suitcase, and we all headed home. My wife and I joked about what happened, and I decided to store the remaining items, with intentions to donate them to Goodwill, the Salvation Army or a homeless shelter the following weekend. However, while preparing to store them, I heard something shifting around in the suitcase, and I reopened it to see what it was. More than anything else, what I found convinced me that Mimi Faust is a complete loser.

Upon reopening the suitcase, I found a stack of documents bound together by paperclip—with Nikko's name—his *real* name Londell Smith—on virtually all of them. Not just any kind of documents, but *serious* stuff that could definitely be used criminally in the wrong hands. These documents consisted of the following:

1. Some of Nikko's personal and business contacts—names and telephone numbers—all written in his *own* handwriting.
2. Information about his Visa Business Card from Bank of America.
3. *Love & Hip Hop: Atlanta*-related Disclosure/Authorization and Guest/Performer Release forms completed by Nikko himself.
4. Nikko's residence history.
5. His actual signature.
6. His Social Security Number.
7. His Driver's License number.
8. An Employer Identification Number that was assigned to him by the IRS for one of his businesses.
9. A Writer's Collaboration Agreement that he signed with Rich Chicks Media, LLC, back in June 2013.

And several other documents that I will not disclose.

After discovering these documents, I lost all of the respect that I *could've* had for Mimi, because we are living in an age in which identity theft, tax fraud and bank fraud are some of the biggest threats that Americans face. Yet, Mimi gave all of this information away as if it was nothing—all because of bitterness and emotion. But the worst part of it all is that *she gave it to people that she did not even know.* That was not only low down and dirty, but also the epitome of stupidity, due to the sensitive nature of the information. I know people who know people, and the people they know told them to tell me that people are paying top-dollar for this kind of information. Fortunately, for Nikko, I just happen to be a *solid* individual, and I have spent almost a thousand dollars making sure these documents remain stored in a secure location, with the intention of someday handing them over to Nikko myself. No games, no ulterior motives— just a gift from one man to another.

But it is shit like this that, in my opinion, makes Mimi a loser. Instead of just letting go and moving on after her split with Nikko, it seems as if she still wanted to hurt him in some way, which is why she gave us the man's personal belongings in the first place. As many people would argue, this proves that she does not have the temperament to excel at the game of power, because her worst enemy would be her own emotions. I have the utmost respect for producer Stevie J., her child's father, but I feel sorry for him too, because who is to say that she would not do the same to him—or even worse? Of all the people on *Love & Hip Hop: Atlanta*, I respect K. Michelle and Joseline Hernandez the most, because strategy comes *natural* to them, and they are shrewd power players even when at their worst. They both think BIG, have BIG personalities, and stick to their guns. So, it is hard for one *not* to respect them. As for Mimi, I have spent enough time around her, off camera, to gauge her psychology. My assessment? She is cool and sweet, when she wants to be. However, there is a bitter, selfish, attention-seeking, oversensitive, overemotional, bougie, artificial side to her that is unmistakable when there are no cameras around. She seems too self-absorbed to think BIG, and her life seems to revolve around a Reality TV show. People like this never truly gain power, because they relegate themselves to certain realms that hamper strategy, seduction and maneuverability. Machiavellian-minded individuals are the complete opposite, and they are far from petty. They keep their minds focused on where they are going, and on everything that has to be *done* in order for them to get there. They simply do not have time for anything else. The point is that true masters go hard all day, every day, and we should all do the same if we want power. If not, eventually, all of our goals and dreams will end up in a graveyard—just like we will.

STEP 6

*Realize that you **have no competition, because Creators create, and competitors compete for what has already been created.***

One of the biggest lies that prevents a person's mind from attaining mastermind status is the notion of competition because, by definition, competition refers to those who aim to do what other people are already doing. This notion has never appealed to me at all. For as long as I can remember, no matter where I go, I *always* stand out, and I do this naturally, because I have always been *different*. This is often seen in my demeanor. I have been called "weird" and "crazy" so many times that I now regard the words with admiration. And I have never been the "monkey see, monkey do" type, because I am more interested in creating loopholes that can get me to my goals faster. If I do something, I have to do it in a way that has never been done before, period. That is what Creators *do*.

In college, they teach us backwards when they teach us about business. They tell us things like, "Business is all about competition," and "Other businesses are your competitors." And, then, later, they also tell us, "Most small businesses fail." Instead of noticing how competition *causes* most small businesses to fail, instead, they try to find a million *other* reasons to substantiate this claim. However, when you really think about it, none of it really adds up. For example, look at it this way. Let us say, hypothetically, that there is a town with 1,000 small businesses established. Of this 1,000, 200 sell footwear; 200 sell cellular phones; 200 sell clothing of all types; 200 sell food; and the remaining 200 sell computers. Each business in each group of 200 is competing with all of the others inside of its group for consumers who buy their products. And all five groups of 200 are competing for customers in general, most of whom have some kind of need for *all* of the products on the market. Then, some new guy moves into town and opens a business, but he is not selling anything that the others are selling—he is selling *guns with custom stocks and handles*. In one year's time, who do you think will have made the most money? Hands down, the guy with the guns. Why? Because he is selling something different that the town is not used to having around, something that virtually everybody *needs*, and something creative. He is just one man, but they represent a thousand businesses. He may only buy a few products from them, but they will flock to him for the new product that he is selling. This means that they will spend more money with him than he will with them and, in the end, he will have made more money. While they were busy competing amongst each other, he had no one to compete with but himself. He *created* an opportunity for himself—and the rest is history.

When someone creates something new or does something in a uniquely creative way that has never really been seen before, the spotlight eventually becomes theirs, because the thing that they create or do breaks the mold of the ordinary. When knives, daggers, swords and arrows were man's primary weapons of choice, those who created the firearm got rich—BIG time. Do you see my point? You were *born* to create, not to compete. If all of your attempts to succeed have being failing, it is probably because you are in the wrong state of mind, too focused on "beating the competition." The truth of the matter, though, is that you *have* no competition. If you handle your business correctly, letting your passion and instincts guide you, and keep your mind focused on either creating something new or doing something old or common in a creatively new way, you will most likely receive different results that bring about success. That was the difference between former heroin kingpin Frank Lucas and his "competitors" back in the late 1960s and early 1970s. His "brand" was purer, had a name that creatively alluded to this in a seemingly mystical way ("Blue Magic"), and people started flocking to it in multitudes. While other dealers were giving stupid names to their "products" and going through intermediaries to acquire them, Lucas was ordering directly from his source in the Golden Triangle and having them delivered to America in casket pallets. Talk about creative! He even surpassed a few Mafia members, some of whom had to buy from him. See, if you want to succeed, you have to approach power and success with this frame of mind. Even though Lucas turned out to be a snitch, which is the only problem I have with the man, the power of his creative mind cannot be underrated. He thought BIG, believed he could pull off his master plan, did so *creatively*—and got rich, with a decent degree of power. With the product he had, there was no *room* for competition. If a *snitch* can get creative and acquire fame, wealth, power and influence, just imagine what *YOU* can do! Be creative, and you will not even *have* to compete. All you have to do is understand the difference and go for it!

STEP 7

Do not allow organized religion to **brainwash** *you.*
Extract from it only the practical knowledge and

wisdom that can make your life more fulfilling, and discard the rest, without exception.

I will not expound much on organized religion, except to point out what many of us either already know or suspect: it uses fear and indoctrination to control minds. The proof about this on historical record, and modern evidence on public record about it as well, is enough to obliterate any debate on this subject. We all know what *really* goes on in the Church, so there is really no need to talk about it. And there is enough information on television to give you a general idea of what is going on with most other religions outside of Christianity. But, in terms of the "Holy Books," where wisdom-based scriptures and passages are concerned, there is not really much of a problem, because these particular parts of the books aim to enlighten the human mind. To all of this, I say, if power is what you want, if you are not deliberately *using* organized religion as a platform to acquire it, then, take from it wisdom only, and random other practical information that you can use to better your life—and discard the rest. If not, inevitably, it will weaken your mind and make you too soft for power. This is why it is called "organized" religion. That which is "organized" is placed under *control*. Religion will only limit your maneuverability, so do not fall for the hype. Besides, if you really pay attention, eventually, you will notice that the highest-ranking members of *any* religion are usually masterminds themselves. Many of them are just confused. If you want to live peacefully, love your enemies, forgive everybody, turn the other cheek, die and, then, go to "heaven," by all means, go to church. But do not look for me when you get there, except every now and then. There is a difference between God and religion. If God is the Ultimate Creator, and religion is a product of man, who was made in *His* image, then, it would benefit you more to spend most of your time with God than man. And you can do this without spending the bulk of your time inside of a building among hypocrites who *say* that they are "fellowshipping" with God, though their actions do not even show it. I am telling you, if you are trying to be BIG in life, stay away from organized religion. You can do whatever you want to do after you make it but, until then, keep your eye on the prize.

STEP 8

Read the following books, all of them, page by page, from cover to cover, and absorb and apply the information within them as if your life depends on it.

There is no doubt about it: books have the power to change lives. As the old saying goes, "experience is the best teacher." What most people do not realize, however, is that experience goes well beyond the personal realm. While personal experience has its advantages, the countless experiences of people throughout human history can teach us lessons that would take us forever to learn on our own. And this is what makes books so important and essential to human development, especially those of the nonfiction variety. Millions of people can attest to how books have changed their lives forever, many of whom can also affirm that something they once learned inside of a book greatly attributed to their acquisition of power and wealth. Because of this, the power of books should never be underestimated. What people fail to read could set them back an entire lifetime. People are so illiterate these days that, if someone wanted to hide something from them, all they would have to do is just put it in a book. This is why it is so important for power pursuers to soak up as much knowledge and wisdom as they can. Armed with the sagacity of the ages, they would be ahead of their time, and on top of their game—making the acquisition of power as sweet as it could ever be. Therefore, in order to help expedite the power process, I have compiled a list of books that, if read and applied thoroughly, could make readers political masterminds in much less time than is usually required. If you open your mind, digest them and start putting what you learn into practice, without doubt or fear, and without procrastination and distraction, while you are still making your way through the list, your life will begin to change before your eyes—as many of the people around you will bear witness. All you have to do is take the initial step, and everything else will follow. If you can bring yourself to do this, then, you are *already* in a position of power, because something so powerful is about to happen to your mind that, at first, even *you* will not believe it—until the results convince you otherwise.

One final word of advice: As you are acquiring these books, do not do what most undetermined people do and just "read" them—*study* them.

Highlight the stuff that stands out to you most. Define words that you may not understand. Compile notes, even *inside* the books, if you have to—if you are the tangible-book-reading type. *Just get involved!* And, even if you have already read, and are already familiar, with some of them, read them *again*. What you did not know and understand then, you know and understand now. The time and energy you put into these books will determine how fast or slowly your life will begin to change, and this is why interaction on your part is so important. Too many people who claim they want to become successful think that all they have to do is skim over book matter in order to gain awareness and understanding, and this is so far from the truth that it is ridiculous. This is what Jay-Z was talking about on his "Renegade" record, featuring Eminem, when he asked, "Do you fools 'listen' to music, or do you just skim through it?" Speed-reading is not the way to go, believe me. I know people with extensive personal libraries who seem knowledgeable on the surface but do not know shit, because they have spent too much time skimming over information that they cannot even remember anymore. Do not fall into this trap. Read these books as if your *life* depended on it because, if you are not where you want to be, or are currently heading there, your life actually does. The decisions you make from this point on will seriously determine where you end up, so do not take this lightly. Give it your *all*, and get the haters, procrastinators, small thinkers and energy vampires out of your life. And, whatever you do, do not even let them know what you are doing, because they will only be waiting for you to fail. However, if you cannot escape them for some reason, and they insist on talking to you about the "new thing" that you are doing (thinking BIG), just downplay it and "keep it moving." They will begin to *see* power and success in your demeanor, and will try to do everything in their power to squash it. Some will talk negatively about what you are reading and doing, in an attempt to instill doubt in you and hinder your success. Others will be even bolder and deliberately spark arguments with you with the intention of throwing you off your game. This is just some of the stuff that you will have to go through when you start thinking BIG amongst *small* people. However, if you can deal with this without losing focus, then, you will be okay. With that said, let us now get to the books!

The 12-Book Blueprint for Power

Aside from the one that you are perusing now, here are the 12 books that will, if thoroughly studied and applied, make you a *huge*-thinking, seductive, power- and success-attaining, Machiavellian mastermind. Each individual book has its own degree of power but, collectively, their power becomes *supreme*. As aforementioned, whether you have already "read" or heard about them before does not matter. Read them *again*, read them NOW, and watch what happens.

It is not what you read that will make you powerful, but rather what you seriously and shrewdly *apply*. Moreover, this particular literary concoction is extraordinary, in the remarkable sense. Once you initiate the power process by turning the first page in the first book, soon after, you will see exactly what I mean. Anyway, here are the books, which I refer to as "Power Scrolls." If power, success, wealth, influence and a mastermind mindset are what you truly want, make it your mission to acquire every single one of them, and never let anyone convince you otherwise.

Power Scroll #1
The Science of Getting Rich
By Wallace D. Wattles

Power Scroll #2
The Magic of Thinking Big
By David J. Schwartz, PhD

Power Scroll #3
The Secret
By Rhonda Byrne

Power Scroll #4
Think Big and Kick Ass in Business and Life
By Bill Zanker and Donald Trump

Power Scroll #5
Money, and the Law of Attraction
By Esther and Jerry Hicks

Power Scroll #6
The Prince
By Niccolò Machiavelli

Power Scroll #7
The Art of War
By Sun Tzu

Power Scrolls 8-11
The Art of Seduction, The 48 Laws of Power,
The 33 Strategies of War, Mastery
By Robert Greene

Power Scroll #12
The 50ᵗʰ Law
By 50 Cent and Robert Greene

From here on out, consider these "Power Scrolls" your collective guide to success. By reading them in the exact order in which they are listed, as opposed to bouncing around in no particular order at all, something powerful will happen to your mind. I cannot explain it, but you will definitely see and experience this for yourself. With each "scroll" that you complete, your intelligence will soar to new heights, your attraction power will increase, and your understanding of human psychology will become more and more profound. And, believe me, by the time that you are done with Scroll #12, you will either be in possession of, or have direct access to, something that will change the course of your life forever. An undeniably great, profitable *idea*; an actual, new, innovative *product*; a master plan that you had *never* even seen coming; or a person who happened to pop up in your life, seemingly "out of the blue," that will guide or point you directly to success. All you will have to do then is take action, and the rest will be history. Some of these things may even overlap, and some of you will be so focused that your abundance will come long before you even *make* it to Scroll #12. The harder you go with the Scrolls, the faster your results. This is just how the Universe works.

* * * * * *

At any rate, political masterminds come and go. Most of the time, we just do not realize what they are when they make a huge splash on the political scene. While widespread conventionalism wants us to believe that politics concern that of government, those who are *excelling* in government are employing strategies based on *true* political reality, which deals with power and the manipulation of human behavior via psychology. In any civilization, seduction, war and strategy constitute a way of life, and mastery of these things enables one to rise to the heights of power. The Machiavellian mindset is the mindset of a master, and the hunger of a master makes it possible for him to do and accomplish the impossible. Donald Trump has broken the political mold, and he proudly stands before us as a testament to the power of mastermind excellence. For this alone, he is due praise. It is time for America to wake up!

No matter what happens on Election Day, the fact remains that Donald Trump has already made his mark on America. His ascension to the top of American politics has given birth to a new political dynamic that will go on to change the very fabric of the United States. The small- thinking days are over, and a BIG-thinking era has just begun. Millions of Americans now know the truth about political corruption at his highest echelons, and The People are no longer awaiting a political messiah—they know that they can become such themselves. The system is rigged, and there is no getting around this. With this now known to the majority, America is on the brink of reconstruction.

Moreover, above all, one thing is certain: If Donald Trump is elected, America *will* become great again! Any Machiavellian mastermind with the ability to build, run and sustain a powerful, successful empire can run a nation. All he needs is the right team, and practicality is ten times better than bureaucracy is on a bad day. Hillary Clinton has virtually *no* experience running *any* kind of empire—she only knows how to play second fiddle to one. In the real world, it is not about where one has *been*, but rather what one can *do*, that matters. And the only thing that she has ever truly done is follow executive orders, because she has never really been in a position to make them herself. If threatened, we *know* that Trump would crush our enemies. We *know* that he has mastered the art of the deal. We *know* that he can create jobs. We *know* that he does not need our money. And, most importantly, we *know* that he truly loves his country. There is no question about any of this. As for his opponent, on the other hand, about her, we cannot be certain. Electing Clinton to the presidency would be like selecting Snuffleupagus for a lead role in *Blade*. This is just my opinion, but it is exactly how I see it. A few presidential terms from now, she would probably be perfect for America. Right now is just not the time.

Lastly, to those of you who want to be rich, who want power, I say to you: If you are smart enough to see through all of this formal, political bullshit this season, then, you already know what you have to do. In the meantime, use Trump's ground-shaking success as motivation and inspiration; focus on reaching your goals and accomplishing your dreams; and go *hard*. The ill wisdom of the ages holds no weight amongst those who are determined to rise. Once you put it into your mind, the thought that you are going to succeed, and you shoot off like a rocket in pursuit of your goal, eventually success will be yours. Male, female or transgender, it all works the same. A year from now, elected or not, Donald Trump will *still* be a billionaire. Where do *you* want to be? What do *you* want to do? Because *you* can be a political mastermind too! Believe it!

Afterword

Writing this book has been an amazing experience, from start to finish. And, for three and a half months, aside from writing, I have been watching Donald Trump's domination of media and politics with an "I told you so" mentality that only a *mastermind* would understand. When I began writing back in May, Trump was not yet the Republican presidential nominee, and had not yet been endorsed by Paul Ryan. However, I projected both his nomination and Ryan's endorsement early on in my manuscript. When these things came to pass, it became clear to certain people around me that I was on to something. The more I wrote, the more Trump's behavior, actions and success proved that I was right, which sent me back to my early chapters countless times, causing me to turn old projections into current facts. Now, as this book goes into production, The Donald is still at it, going as hard as ever on his quest to help make America great again. He is *still* shaking up things, *still* Machiavellian, and still *winning*—in spite of what some questionable polls and one-sided reporters are saying about him in liberal media. However, before I officially close, I would like to make a few additional points concerning the recent Hillary Clinton email controversy, Trump's newest campaign changes, and how Trump can get a sizeable portion of the black vote, in order to keep this work as current as possible before its release—and before November. With that said, here are my final thoughts, in brief.

At this point, after all of the documents that have been leaked, I think it would be stupid for anybody to say that Hillary did not do anything wrong. As Scott Amy, member of the Project On Government Oversight, recently said in a CNN interview, "Government employees have an obligation to avoid even the appearance of a conflict of interest." Yet, in these emails, from what I have seen, some of those who donated the most money to Clinton's foundation receive "favors." This raises the following question: If Hillary were elected as president, and one of our enemies, or one of their allies, decided to donate millions to her foundation in an effort to "buy" her, could she be bought? To be honest, I think that she *could*—it is common sense. And any president who can be bought not only cannot be trusted, but is also a potential *treasonist*, plain and simple.

As for Trump's campaign, I recently read that he is making some essential changes to it that will put him in a better position to win in his debates against Hillary and clench the presidency in November—all while being *himself*. The "presidential" thing, by conventional definition, is just not him, which would only limit his chances at winning, because Trump being Trump is what has gotten him this far in the first place. He is being *somewhat* presidential—just in his own way. I believe that his performance during the debates will shock the world, because people have a certain perception of him, especially Hillary Clinton. If they are not careful, their underestimation of him will only serve him the White House on a platter.

As for black votes, all Trump truly needs is a black face on the ground with *integrity*, who can reach the African American demographic in a unique way that is not colored by political ideology. He needs someone young and unconventional with flavor, intelligence and *flaws*— because this particular demographic is not impressed by uppity-appearing, black Republicans in suits. The Trump message has to come to them raw and uncut, with an emphasis on what can be done for *them*. And it actually has to be *done*. If Trump could find someone like this to deliver his message, in November, black votes would pour in for him in *droves*. It is not *what* you do, it is *how* you do it, as the old saying goes, and the African American community has to be appealed to in a certain way. Otherwise, the Trump campaign will *never* reach them. Believe me.

All in all, I believe that Trump has done an amazing job in his pursuit of presidential power, and there is still much more to come. By keeping your mind focused on strategy, power, war and seduction, you will come to find that nothing he does will surprise you—it would only make you *respect* him. Donald Trump is a mastermind and, if you do not understand this now, eventually, you will. I just hope that, whenever that time comes, Hillary Clinton is not President. But, if so, god help us all.

About the Author

A native of New Orleans, Louisiana, Niccolò DaVinci is an independent political strategist and humanologist. A Donald Trump aficionado, he holds an associate degree with an emphasis in General Business, and is a public speaker and former member of both Toastmasters International and the United States Junior Chamber of Commerce. He is also an intermediate Spanish translator and Boys Town-certified, Educational American Sign Language interpreter with an unbelievable connection to CNN correspondent Rosa Flores. He lives with his wife, Sheron, in Marietta, Georgia.

DaVinci loves to receive feedback from his readers, and anyone who would like to contact him, for purposes of feedback or otherwise, can do so via email at www.niccolodavinci9@gmail.com. Or you can simply friend, follow or message him on Facebook at: www.facebook.com/niccolo.davinci.1.